VOGUE® KNITTING

CROCHETED SHAWLS

on the go!™

VOGUE® KNITTING

CROCHETED SHAWLS

SIXTH&SPRING BOOKS
NEW YORK

SIXTH&SPRING BOOKS
233 Spring Street
New York, New York 10013

Library of Congress Cataloging-in-Publication Data
Library of Congress Control Number: 2007920931

ISBN-10: 1-933027-24-X
ISBN-13: 978-1-933027-24-1

Manufactured in China

3 5 7 9 10 8 6 4 2

First Edition, 2007

TABLE OF CONTENTS

INTRODUCTION

What do you get when you pair crafting's hottest trend with a timelessly chic fashion accessory? Fabulous crocheted shawls! The *On the Go!* collection you have in your hands features this favorite wardrobe staple in just about every style, from fun and flirty to classically sophisticated to unique and funky.

Worn as a functional cover-up or a deliberate fashion statement, a shawl is the perfect addition to any outfit, and these projects utilize an assortment of materials including ribbon, mohair, baby alpaca and cashmere, so you can crochet a shawl for every occasion and every season. Plus, shawls make great gifts with no need to worry about individual measurements; these stunners will wrap, drape or tie beautifully on anyone!

Both newbie crocheters and experienced veterans will appreciate the variety of patterns included. Whether made with classic crochet techniques like granny squares and medallions or more innovative stitch patterns such as an eye-catching four-leaf clover design or cozy crocheted cables, each shawl is a treasure in its own right.

Crocheted Shawls is sure to become a favorite of your knitting library. Grab your hook and let yourself get wrapped up; it's time to **CROCHET ON THE GO!**

THE BASICS

While many crafters consider crochet a family tradition, few may realize that it is a practice dating back to ancient times. Shepherds were probably the first to crochet, using hooked sticks to turn their spun wool scraps into clothes. By the sixteenth century, Irish nuns were using bone and ivory hooks to create lace patterns that crocheters still make today. And in the nineteenth century, the aspirational middle classes learned the craft in imitation of society's elite, who were educated in such handwork. So crochet became part of popular culture, a practical and artistic craft that anyone could do.

Lately, word is that crochet has made a comeback; history, though, tells us it never really left. People are just exploring new hobbies, rediscovering old skills and expanding their knowledge of handcrafts. Our aim is to encourage and entice a whole spectrum of crocheters, whatever their experience, with this book. What is the next step up from the basic crocheted scarf? The crocheted shawl. It is simply a little bigger and based on a few different shapes: square, rectangle, triangle and circle. Very little, if any, finishing is required. Shawls are also very versatile: You can wear them as outerwear on those cool days, in the office to keep the chill off or to dress up an evening outfit. We have chosen a variety of styles and skill levels in this book to entice every crocheter. And because they are mostly quick and easy to make, they are perfect for giving as gifts.

Crochet is accessible and really quite easy to learn. Stitches are formed by pulling loops through other loops, or stitches, with a hook, creating the simple chain that is used in all patterns. Unlike in knitting, there is no balancing act with needles, shifting stitches from one needle to another. In crochet, one hand and one hook do all the work, and the finished fabric lies away from the hook, letting crocheters concentrate on only the next stitch they need to make. And, unlike in other crafts, correcting a mistake is fairly stress-free; simply tug on the yarn to easily pull out the stitches you have worked.

GAUGE

Most shawl patterns don't rely on perfect fit as a garment does, but it is still important to crochet a gauge swatch. Measure gauge as illustrated here. (Launder and block your gauge swatch before taking measurements). Try different hook sizes until your sample measures the required number of stitches and rows. To get fewer stitches to the inch/cm, use larger hooks; to get more stitches to the inch/cm, use smaller needles. It's a good idea to keep your gauge swatch to test embroidery, embellishments or blocking and cleaning methods.

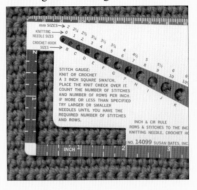

In crochet, finished pieces have unique characteristics. The combination of chains and joinings in crochet creates a sheer netting, whose airiness can dress up an outfit or just add a dash of style. Other times, the depth of the garment, depending on the chosen yarn, can actually take on a rich three-dimensional appearance. And it is just as easy to learn to finish crochet. Though crocheted pieces often lack stretchability, again, depending on the yarn used, they usually

CROCHET HOOKS					
U.S.	Metric	U.S.	Metric	U.S.	Metric
14 steel	.60mm	C/2	2.50mm	I/9	5.50mm
12 steel	.75mm	D/3	3.00mm	J/10	6.00mm
10 steel	1.00mm	E/4	3.50mm		6.50mm
6 steel	1.50mm	F/5	4.00mm	K/10.5	7.00mm
5 steel	1.75mm	G/6	4.50mm		
B/1	2.00mm	H/8	5.00mm		

lie flat without further blocking or finishing.

We hope that by now, you are eager to pick up a hook and start to crochet. If not, take a look at the pieces in this dynamic collection; in no time you will be exploring and enjoying the fresh, contemporary styles that have emerged from an ancient tradition.

If you're not convinced that it's easy to learn to crochet, perhaps the shawls in this book will inspire you. They run the gamut from basic to more complicated stitches, giving experienced crocheters ample challenge and offering novices the chance to graduate to more difficult projects as they progress. The easy shawl styles, such as the Loopy Shawl on page 34 and the Mondrian Shawl on page 82, often have a simple one-row repeat and work up quickly with a large hook and bulky weight yarn. Such basic patterns let the yarn take center stage. Meanwhile, the more advanced designs, like the Snowflake Shawl on page 56, the Openwork Shawl on page 70 and the Aran Shawl on page 86 do not necessarily have more difficult stitch techniques; rather the instructions, with their series of repeats and pattern layouts, require more concentration to create the perfect piece.

CONSTRUCTION

There is very little to the construction of most shawls, as they are usually worked in one piece with little or no shaping. However, some more complicated patterns have more than one piece, such as the Medallion Shawl on page 31, the Star Shawl on page 44, the Spiraled Flower Shawl on page 47 and the Circles Shawl on page 75.

SIZING

The shawls in this book are written in one size. If you are not sure if the size given in the pattern will fit you, then look at the "Finished Measurements" at the beginning of the pattern, cut or fold a piece of fabric to those measurements, try it on, and adjust from there. It is relatively easy to change the measurements. If the style is a simple rectangle or square, add or subtract chains to the foundation chain to alter the width (pay attention to the stitch multiple, if necessary), and work fewer or more rows to alter the length. For a triangle shape, it is a more involved process. If the triangle begins at the widest point, you will have to adjust the number of stitches on the foundation chain. First determine the desired width and alter the number of foundation chain stitches accordingly. Then decide on the length to

Categories of yarn, gauge ranges and recommended needle and hook sizes

Yarn Weight Symbol & Category Names	**1** Super Fine	**2** Fine	**3** Light	**4** Medium	**5** Bulky	**6** Super Bulky
Type of Yarns in Category	Sock, Fingering, Baby	Sport, Baby	DK, Light Worsted	Worsted, Afghan, Aran	Chunky, Craft, Rug	Bulky, Roving
Knit Gauge Range* in Stockinette Stitch to 4 Inches	27–32 sts	23–26 sts	21–24 sts	16–20 sts	12–15 sts	6–11 sts
Recommended Needle in Metric Size Range	2.25–3.25 mm	3.25–3.75 mm	3.75–4.5 mm	4.5–5.5 mm	5.5–8 mm	8 mm and larger
Recommended Needle U.S. Size Range	1 to 3	3 to 5	5 to 7	7 to 9	9 to 11	11 and larger
Crochet Gauge* Ranges in Single Crochet To 4 Inches	21–32 sts	16–20 sts	12–17 sts	11–14 sts	8–11 sts	5–9 sts
Recommended Hook in Metric Size Range	2.25–3.5 mm	3.5–4.5 mm	4.5–5.5 mm	5.5–6.5 mm	6.5–9 mm	9 mm and larger
Recommended Hook U.S. Size Range	B–1 to E–4	E–4 to 7	7 to I–9	I–9 to K–10½	K–10½ to M–13	M–13 and larger

*Guidelines only: The above reflects the most commonly used needle or hook sizes for specific yarn categories.

SKILL LEVELS FOR CROCHET

Beginner
Ideal first project.

Very Easy Very Vogue
Basic stitches, minimal shaping, simple finishing.

Intermediate
For crocheters with some experience. More intricate stitches, shaping and finishing.

Experienced
For crocheters able to work patterns with complicated shaping and finishing.

the point, calculate the number of rows needed to get to the point, and work the decreases evenly over this number of rows. Of course, if the triangle is worked from the point up, you still need to determine the width and length, but you also need to reverse the shaping. That is, chain the same number of stitches as in the original pattern and adjust the increases. Also note that if you adjust any pattern from the original, you may need to alter the yarn amount.

YARN SELECTION

For an exact reproduction of the projects shown in this book, use the yarn listed in the Materials section of the pattern. We've chosen yarns that are readily available in the U.S. and Canada at the time of printing. The Resources list on pages 90 and 91 provides addresses of yarn distributors. Contact them for the name of a retailer in your area.

YARN SUBSTITUTION

You may wish to substitute yarns. Perhaps a spectacular yarn matches your new dress or slacks; maybe you view small-scale projects as a chance to incorporate leftovers from your yarn stash; or it may be that the yarn specified is not available in your area. Shawls allow you to be as creative as you like, but you'll need to crochet to the given gauge to obtain the finished measurements with the substitute yarn. Be sure to consider how the fiber content of the substitute yarn will affect the comfort and the ease of care of your projects. To facilitate yarn substitution, *Vogue Knitting* grades yarn by the standard stitch gauge obtained in single crochet. You'll find a grading number in the Materials section of the pattern, immediately following the fiber type of the yarn. Look for a substitute yarn that falls into the same category. The suggested hook size and gauge on the yarn label should be comparable to that on the Standard Yarn Weight chart (see page 13). You'll need to crochet to the given gauge to obtain the crocheted measurements with a substitute yarn (see "Gauge" on page 11). Make pattern adjustments where necessary. Be sure to consider how different yarn types (chenille, mohair, bouclé, etc.) will affect the final appearance of your shawl and how they will feel against your skin. Also take fiber care into consideration: Some yarns can be machine or hand-washed; others will require dry cleaning.

After you've successfully gauge-swatched a substitute yarn, you'll need to determine how much of the substitute yarn the project requires. First, find the total yardage of the original yarn in the pattern by multiplying the number of balls by yards/meters per ball. Divide this figure by the new yards/meters per ball listed on the ball band. Round up to the next whole number. The result is the number of balls required.

READING CROCHET INSTRUCTIONS

If you are used to reading knitting instructions, then crochet instructions may seem a little tedious to follow. Crochet instructions use more abbreviations and punctuation and fewer words than traditional knitting instructions. Along with the separation of stitches and use of brackets, parentheses, commas and other punctuation, numerous repetitions may occur within a single row or round. Therefore, you must pay close attention to reading instructions while you crochet. Here are a few explanations of the more common terms used in this book.

Use of Parentheses ( )

Sometimes parentheses are used to indicate stitches that are to be worked all into one stitch such as "in next st work ( )" or "( ) in next st."

First st, Next st

The beginning stitch of every row is referred to as the "first st." When counting the turning chain (t-ch) as one stitch, the row or round will begin by instructing that you work into the next st (that is, skip the first st or space or whatever is designated in the pattern).

Stitch Counts

Sometimes the turning chain that is worked at the end (or beginning) of a row or a round will be referred to as 1 stitch, and it is then included in the stitch count. In those cases, you will work into the next stitch, thus skipping the first stitch of the row or round. When the turning chain is not counted as a stitch, work into the first actual stitch.

Stitches Described

Sometimes the stitches are described as sc, dc, tr, ch-2 loop, 2-dc group, etc., and sometimes, such as in a mesh pattern of sc, ch 1-each sc and each ch 1 will be referred to as a st.

Back Loop

Along the top of each crochet stitch or chain there are two loops. The loop furthest away from you is the "back loop."

Front Loop

Along the top of each crochet stitch or chain there are two loops. The loop closest to you is the "front loop."

Joining New Colors

When joining new colors in crochet, whether at the beginning of a row or while working across, always work the stitch in the old color to the last 2 loops, then draw the new color through the last 2 loops and continue with the new color.

Working Over Ends

Crochet has a unique flat top along each row that is perfect for laying the old color across and working over the ends for several stitches. This will alleviate the need to cut and weave in ends later.

Form a Ring

When a pattern is worked in the round, as in a square, medallion or flower, the beginning chains are usually closed into a ring by working a slip stitch into the first chain. Then on the first round, stitches are usually worked into the ring and less often into each chain.

FOLLOWING CHARTS

Charts are a convenient way to follow colorwork, lace, cable and other stitch patterns at a glance. *Vogue Knitting* stitch charts utilize the universal crocheting language of "symbolcraft." When crocheting back and forth in rows, read charts from right to left on right-side (RS) rows and from left to right on wrong-side (WS) rows, repeating any stitch and row repeats as directed in the pattern. When crocheting in the round, read charts from right to left on every round. Posting a self-adhesive note under your working row is an easy way to keep track of your place on a chart.

BLOCKING

Blocking crochet is usually not necessary. However, in those cases when you do need to smooth out the fabric, choose a blocking method consistent with information on the yarn care label and always test your gauge swatch. Note that some yarns, such as chenilles and ribbons, do not benefit from blocking. Choose a blocking method according to the yarn-care label and always test-block your gauge swatch.

Wet Block Method

Using rustproof pins, pin pieces to measurements on a flat surface and lightly dampen using a spray bottle. Allow to dry before removing pins.

Steam Block Method

Pin shawl to measurements with wrong side of the fabric facing up. Steam lightly, holding the iron 2"/5cm above the crocheting. Do not press the iron directly onto the piece, as it will flatten the stitches.

FINISHING

After blocking, there is very little, if any, finishing on a shawl. Many times fringe is added to the ends. You can make the fringe as short or long as you like, depending on preference or amount of leftover yarn. A crocheted edge can also be added to keep the edges from curling.

Refer to the yarn label for the recommended cleaning method. Many of the shawls in the book can be washed by hand (or in the machine on a gentle or wool cycle) in lukewarm water with a mild detergent. Do not agitate, and do not soak for more than 10 minutes. Rinse gently with tepid water; then fold in a towel and gently press the water out. Lay flat to dry, away from excessive heat and light.

FRINGE

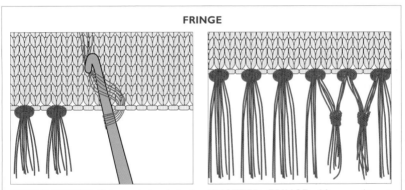

SIMPLE FRINGE: Cut yarn twice desired length plus extra for knotting. On wrong side, insert hook from front to back through piece and over folded yarn. Pull yarn through. Draw ends through and tighten. Trim yarn.

KNOTTED FRINGE: After working a simple fringe (it should be longer to allow for extra knotting), take one half of the strands from each fringe and knot them with half the strands from the neighboring fringe.

CROCHET STITCHES

CHAIN

I *Pass the yarn over the hook and catch it with the hook.*

2 *Draw the yarn through the loop on the hook.*

3 *Repeat steps 1 and 2 to make a chain.*

SINGLE CROCHET

I *Insert the hook through top two loops of a stitch. Pass the yarn over the hook and draw up a loop—two loops on hook.*

2 *Pass the yarn over the hook and draw through both loops on hook.*

3 *Continue in the same way, inserting the hook into each stitch.*

HALF DOUBLE CROCHET

I *Pass the yarn over the hook. Insert the hook through the top two loops of a stitch.*

2 *Pass the yarn over the hook and draw up a loop—three loops on hook. Pass the yarn over the hook.*

3 *Draw through all three loops on hook.*

DOUBLE CROCHET

I *Pass the yarn over the hook. Insert the hook through the top two loops of a stitch.*

2 *Pass the yarn over the hook and draw up a loop— three loops on hook.*

3 *Pass the yarn over the hook and draw it through the first two loops on the hook, pass the yarn over the hook and draw through the remaining two loops. Continue in the same way, inserting the hook into each stitch.*

SLIP STITCH

Insert the crochet hook into a stitch, catch the yarn and pull up a loop. Draw the loop through the loop on the hook.

CROCHET TERMS AND ABBREVIATIONS

approx approximately

beg begin(ning)

CC contrast color

ch chain(s)

cm centimeter(s)

cont continue(ing)

dc double crochet (U.K.: tr—treble)

dec decrease(ing)—reduce the stitches in a row (work stitches together or skip the stitches)

foll follow(s)(ing)

g gram(s)

hdc half double crochet (U.K.: htr—half treble)

inc increase(ing)—add stitches in a row (work extra stitches into a stitch or between the stitches)

LH left-hand

lp(s) loop(s)

m meter(s)

MC main color

mm millimeter(s)

oz ounce(s)

pat(s) patterns

pm place markers—place or attach a loop of contrast yarn or purchased stitch marker as indicated

rem remain(s)(ing)

rep repeat

rnd(s) round(s)

RH right-hand

RS right side(s)

sc single crochet (U.K.: dc—double crochet)

sk skip

sl st slip stitch (U.K.: single crochet)

sp(s) space(s)

st(s) stitch(es)

t-ch turning chain

tog together

tr treble (U.K.: tr tr—triple treble)

WS wrong side(s)

work even continue in pattern without increasing or decreasing (U.K.: work straight)

yd yard(s)

yo yarn over—wrap the yarn around the hook (U.K.: yrh)

*** repeat directions following * as many times as indicated

[ ] repeat directions inside brackets as many times as indicated

MOHAIR SHAWL

Flamenco flair

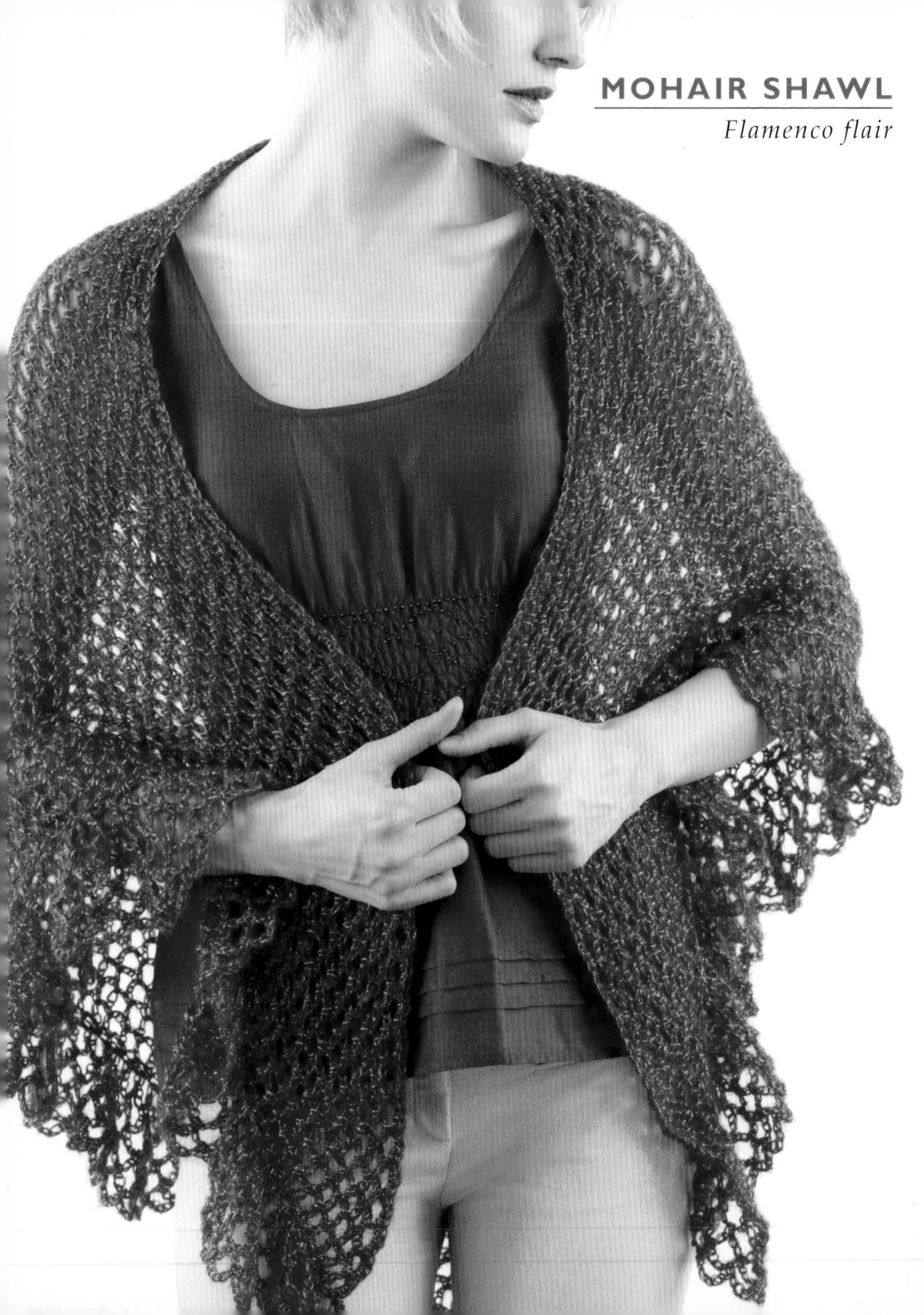

■■■▢

Turn some heads in this Deborah Hedges design. An unexpected combination of mohair and metallic yarns spices things up while an openwork pattern enhanced with a scalloped border keeps it freshly feminine.

SIZES
Instructions are written for one size.

FINISHED MEASUREMENTS
■ Approx 70"/177.5cm wide x 35"/89cm long

MATERIALS
■ 3 ⅞oz/25g balls (each approx 225yd/206m) of Knit One, Crochet Too *Douceur et Soie* (baby mohair/silk) in #8249 deep garnet (A) **2**
■ 3 ⅞oz/25g balls (each approx 224yd/205m) of Knit One, Crochet Too *18 Karat* (rayon/metallized polyester) in #254 poppy gold (D) **1**
■ Size J/10 (6mm) crochet hook *or size to obtain gauge*

GAUGE
5 ch-3 spaces to 4"/10cm.
Take time to check gauge.

SHAWL
Ch 2, join rnd with a sl st in first ch to form a ring.
Row 1 (RS) Ch 3, sc in ch-2 sp, ch 3, sc in same ch-2 sp. Ch 3, turn.
Row 2 Sc in first ch-3 sp, ch 3, sc in next ch-3 sp, ch 3, sc in same ch-3 space—3 ch-3 sps. Ch 3, turn.
Row 3 Sc in first ch-3 sp, *ch 3, sc in next ch-3 sp; rep from * once, ch 3, sc in same ch-3 sp—4 ch-3 sps. Ch 3, turn.
Row 4 Sc in first ch-3 sp, *ch 3, sc in next ch-3 sp; rep from * across to last ch-3 sp, ch 3, sc in same ch-3 sp. Ch 3, turn.
Rows 5–80 Rep row 4—78 ch-3 sps at end of Row 80.
Fasten off.
Border
Row 1 Working across top of shawl, ch 1, 3 sc in each ch-3 sp across to other end; working down side of shawl, ch 5, sc in first ch-3 sp, *ch 5, sc in next ch-3 sp; rep from * down one side and up other side of shawl to beg ch 1, sl st in ch-1 sp. Ch 5, turn.
Row 2 Working down same side as previous rnd and working on side edges only, sc in first ch-5 sp, *ch 5, sc in next ch-5 sp; rep from * down this side and up next side to beg ch-5 sp, sc in beg ch-5 sp. Ch 5, turn.
Rows 3–5 Working down same side as previous rnd and working on side edges only, rep Rnd 2.
Row 6 Working down same side as previous rnd and working on side edges only, rep rnd 2, join with a sl st in beg of previous rnd. Fasten off.

FINISHING
Block shawl lightly to measurements. Weave in ends.

■■■□

In the mood for love? Kristin Omdahl's airy lace shawl, worked in alpaca and silk, will add a hint of romance to any outfit.

SIZES

Instructions are written for one size.

FINISHED MEASUREMENTS

■ Approx 19"/48.5cm wide x 62"/132cm long

MATERIALS

■ 6 1¾oz/50g balls (each approx 146yd/133m) of Blue Sky Alpacas *Alpaca Silk* (alpaca/silk) in #129 amethyst 🌐

■ Size G/6 (4mm) crochet hook *or size to obtain gauge*

■ Size US 17 (12.75mm) knitting needle

■ Yarn needle

GAUGE

16 sc and 8 rows to 4"/10cm in blocked broomstick lace pat.
Take time to check gauge.

SHAWL

Ch 81.

Row 1 Sc into 2nd ch from hook and each ch across—80 sc. Do not turn.

Row 2 Working from left to right, holding knitting needles in left hand, pull up a lp long enough to place onto knitting needle, *insert crochet hook in next st of previous row, pull up a lp long enough to place onto knitting needle; rep from * across—80 lps on knitting needle.

Row 3 Insert crochet hook into first 4 lps on knitting needle, sl st in same sp, ch1, work 4 sc in same sp, *insert crochet hook into next 4 lps and slide off knitting needle, work 4 sc in same sp; rep from * across.

Row 4 Rep row 2.

Rows 5–60 Rep Rows 3 and 4 alternately.

Row 61 Rep row 3.

Fasten off.

Work along opposite side of beg ch, with RS facing, as foll:

Row 1 Sl st in first sc to join yarn, ch1, sc into each sp across—80 sc. Do not turn.

Rows 2–61 Rep rows 2–61 same as for the opposite side.

Do not fasten off.

Edging

Turn shawl 90 degrees and work along edge of rows.

Rnd 1 Work 5 sc in each elongated lp section across, work 3 sc in row-ends along center panel (beg ch), then work 5 sc into each elongated lp section to corner.

Turn shawl 90 degrees and work 1 sc in each sc across working 3 sc in the first and last sc of row.

Turn shawl 90 degrees and work 5 sc in each elongated lp section across, work 3 sc in row-ends along center panel (beg ch), then work 5 sc in each elongated lp section to corner.

Turn shawl 90 degrees and work 1 sc into each sc across working 3 sc into the first and last sc of row. Sl st to first sc of rnd to join.

Rnd 2 Work sc into each sc around, working 3 sc in each corner.

Rnd 3 Rep rnd 2.

Rnd 4 *Work sc in next st, ch 4, sl st into 3rd ch from hook (picot made), sk 1 st; rep from * around, join rnd with a sl st in first sc. Fasten off.

FINISHING

Block shawl lightly to measurements. Weave in ends.

SPIRAL SHAWL

Shawl du soleil

This graceful design by Kristin Omdahl begins with a center spiral and comes full circle with a scalloped picot edging.

SIZES

Instructions are written for one size.

FINISHED MEASUREMENTS

■ Approx 60"/152.5cm in diameter

MATERIALS

■ 15 1¾oz/50g balls (each approx 125yd/114m) of Plymouth Yarn Co. *Baby Alpaca DK* (superfine baby alpaca) in #1104 butter ③

■ Size H/8 (5mm) crochet hook *or size to obtain gauge*

■ Stitch marker

■ Yarn needle

GAUGE

16 tr and 4 rnds to 4"/10cm.
Take time to check gauge.

STITCH GLOSSARY

Triple picot (Ch 4, sl st into 3rd ch from hook) 3 times, then sl st into 1st ch of 1st picot made.

SHAWL

Ch 4, join rnd with a sl st in first ch.
Rnd 1 Work 8 sc into ring.
Rnd 2 Continue in a spiral and work (2 hdc in back lp of next sc) 5 times, (2 dc in back lp of next sc) 3 times, (2 dc in back lp of next hdc) 6 times, (2 tr in back lp of next hdc) 4 times, (2 tr in back lp of next dc) 3 times, (1 tr in back lp of next dc, 2 tr in back lp of next dc) 7 times, 1 tr in back lp of next dc, (2 tr in back lp of next tr, 1 tr in back lp of next tr) 2 times—40 sts when spiral is completed. Place a marker at end of this rnd to denote beg/end of each rnd and move this marker up on each rnd.

Rnd 3 Continuing in a spiral work 2 tr into each st around—80 tr. Do not join at end of rnds.

Next 2 rnds Work tr in each st around.
Next rnd Work 2 tr in each st around—160 tr.

Next 4 rnds Work tr in each st around.
Next rnd Work 2 tr in each st around—320 tr.

Next 8 rnds Work tr in each st around.
Next rnd Work 2 tr in each st around—640 tr.

Next 5 rnds Work tr in each st around.
Over the next 4 sts, work (dc tbl, hdc tbl, sc tbl)**, sl st through both loops—this will be where you pick up later for the spiral piping.

Edging
Note Work through both loops for remainder of shawl.

Rnd 1 Ch 11 (counts as dc and ch 8), sk 5 sts, *dc, ch 8, sk 5 sts; rep from * around, join rnd with a sl st into 3rd ch of beg of rnd.

Rnd 2 Sl st in 1st ch-8 sp, *(sc, hdc, dc, 3 tr, triple picot, 3 tr, dc, hdc, sc) in 1st ch-8 sp; rep from * around in each ch-8 sp, join rnd with a sl st in 1st sc at beg of rnd. Fasten off.

Spiral piping

Join yarn with sl st to free lp of last st worked through back lps only (st noted with ** above). Working in reverse sc (working from left to right) for remainder of shawl, sc in same lp as joining yarn, *ch 1, sk next st to the right, work sc in next st to the right; rep from * until the center of the shawl. Fasten off.

Block shawl lightly to measurements. Weave in ends.

GRANNY SQUARE SHAWL

Blueberry cobbler

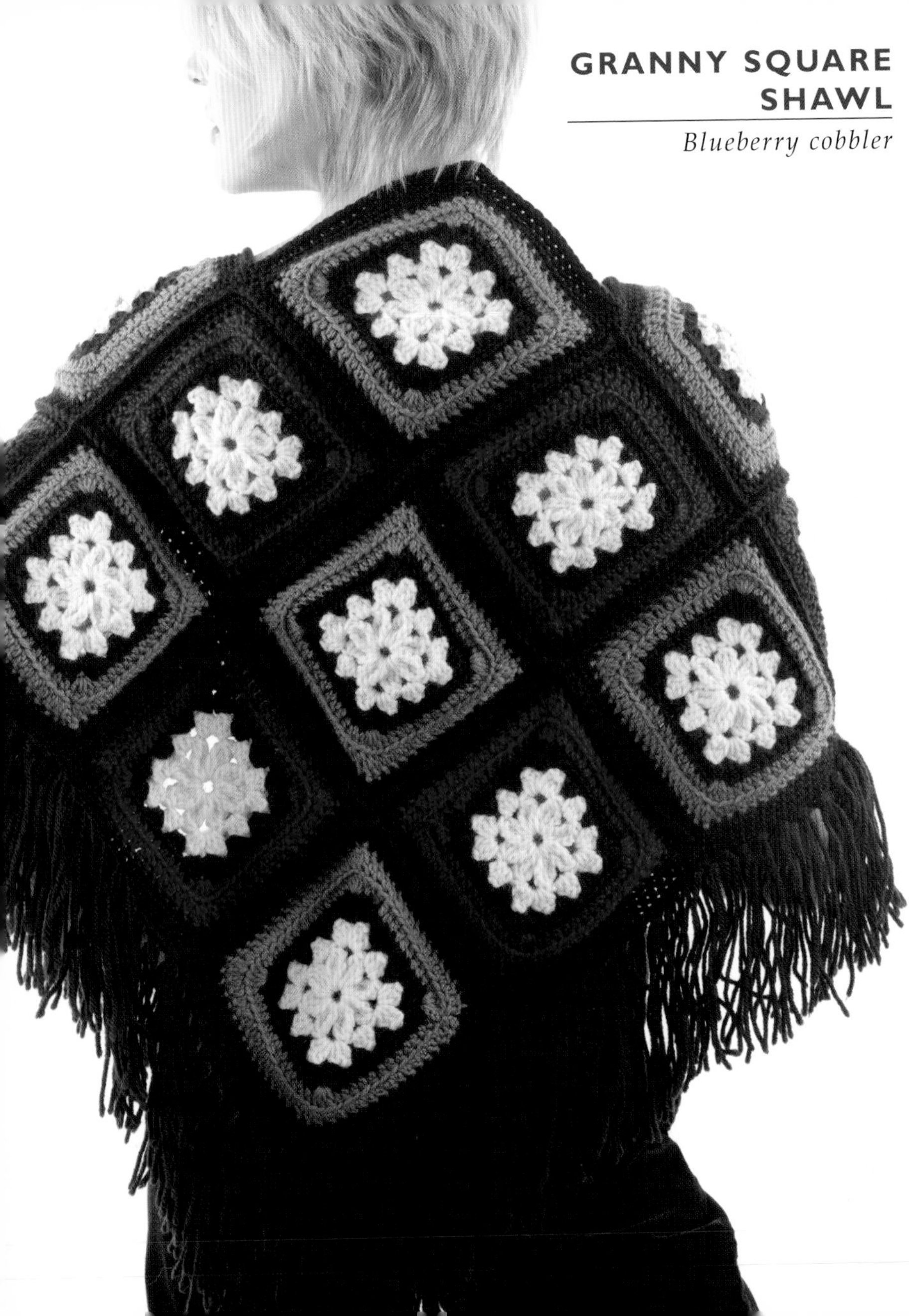

■■■□

Everything old is new again with PD Cagliastro's vintage-chic design. Individual granny squares are assembled in a graduated fashion creating a capelet-like shawl that fastens with crocheted ties.

SIZES

Instructions are written for one size.

FINISHED MEASUREMENTS

■ Approx 25"/63.5cm long x 44"/109cm wide

MATERIALS

■ 1 3oz/85g ball (each approx 158yd/144m) of Lion Brand Yarn *Lion Wool* (wool) in #99 winter white (A), #178 dark teal (B), #123 sage (C) and #111 midnight blue (D) **④**

■ Size H/8 (5mm) crochet hook *or size to obtain gauge*

■ Size C/2 (3mm) crochet hook for finishing

■ Yarn darner

■ Yarn needle (optional)

GAUGE

One square is approx 6"/15cm x 6"/15cm using size H/8 (5mm) crochet hook.
Take time to check gauge.

Notes

1 All rounds, assembly and fringes are worked with right side facing you.

2 Leave long enough tails of each color to weave in during the finishing.

3 Rounds 1–5 are worked into only the back loop of the stitch.

4 Rounds 6 and 7 are worked through both loops of the stitch.

SQUARE C

(make 9)

With A, ch 5, join rnd with a sl st in 1st ch.

Rnd 1 Working into back lp only, ch 4 (counts as 1 tr), keeping last lp of each tr on hook work 2 tr in ring, yo and draw through all 2 lps on hook, ch 3, *keeping last lp of each tr on hook work 3 tr in ring, yo, draw through all 4 lps on hook, ch 3; rep from * 6 times more, join rnd in top of 1st petal with a sl st. Fasten off.

Rnd 2 Join A in any ch-3 sp, ch 3 (counts as 1st dc), (2 dc, ch 2, 3 dc) in same ch-3 sp for corner, 3 dc in next ch-3 sp, *(3 dc, ch 2, 3 dc), in next ch-3 sp, 3 dc in next ch-3 sp; rep from * 2 times more, join rnd in 3rd ch of 1st ch-3 with a sl st. Fasten off.

Rnd 3 Join D in any ch-3 sp, ch 3 (counts as 1st dc), (2 dc, ch 2, 3 dc) in same ch-3 sp, 3 dc in each of next 2 ch-3 sps, *(3 dc, ch 2, 3 dc) in next ch-3 sp, 3 dc in each of next 2 ch-3 sps; rep from * 2 times more, join rnd in 3rd ch of 1st ch-3 with a sl st. Fasten off.

Rnd 4 Join C in any corner sp, ch 3, 3 dc in same sp, dc in next 12 dc, *4 dc in corner sp, dc in next 12 dc; rep from * around, join rnd with a sl st. Fasten off.

Rnd 5 Join C in any corner sp, ch 3, dc in each dc around, join rnd with a sl st. Fasten off.

Rnd 6 Join D in 4th st to the right of any corner, sc in each of next 3 sc, 2 sc in corner, sc in each st around, working 2 sc in each corner, join rnd with a sl st. Do not fasten off.

Rnd 7 With D, rep rnd 6. Fasten off.

SQUARE B

(make 6)

Rep rnds 1–7 of square C. However, work rnds 4 and 5 with B instead of C.

FINISHING

On each square make sure all loose ends are tied off and weave in ends.

ASSEMBLY

This piece is assembled in the following pattern:

Pin all the squares tog as above, carefully lining up the corners. Using D, working through the lps of 2 squares, sc through both squares to attach them OR you can sew the squares tog, carefully matching the sts from one square to another. If you choose to sew them they will not have the ridge that makes this piece unique.

Border

After all squares are attached, starting at the lowest corner and continuing with D, work 3 sc in the point (corner), then sc around the entire shawl and work 3 sc at each point (corner). Work 4 more rnds in this manner, then sl st closed at the point where border was started.

FRINGE

Using D, cut 321 strands of yarn each 11"/28cm long. Use 3 strands for each fringe and start at the lowest point on the shawl with the RS facing you. Attach fringes along lower edge, working left and right of the starting point and skipping 1 st between each fringe, always working through both lps of the st.

TIES

(make 2)

Holding shawl with the 3 non-fringed squares at at top, attach D with 2 sc to the top point of each outer square (skipping the center square), ch 111, leaving a 4"/10cm tail, and fasten off. Using your yarn darner, feed the tail back down through the ch for 1"/2.5cm and trim off. Tie a small knot in the end of the tie.

FINISHING

Block shawl lightly to measurements. Weave in ends. Trim fringe evenly if necessary.

Assembly Diagram

C
B C
C B C
B C B C
C B C B C   lowest point

MEDALLION SHAWL

Grape expectations

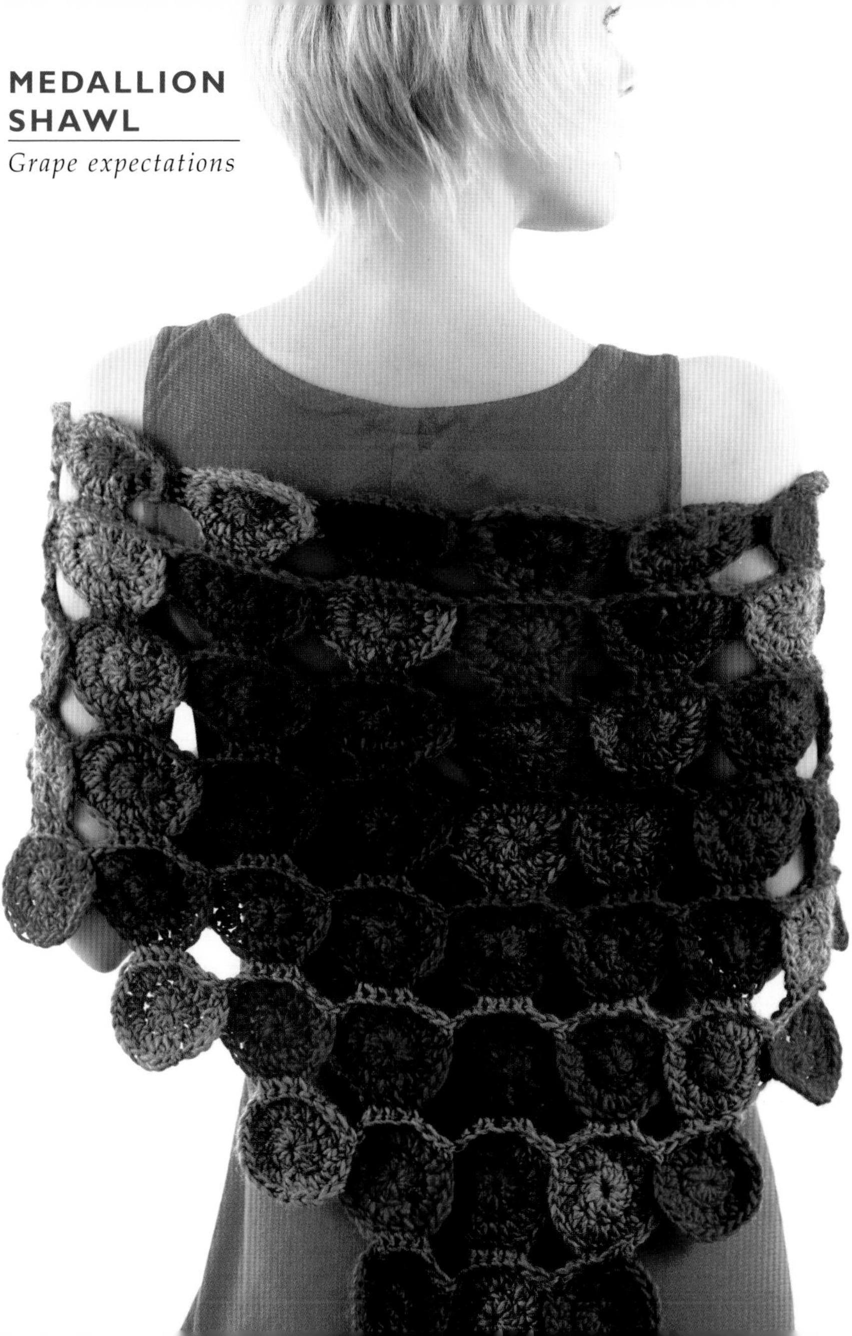

Marty Miller's stylish shawl will have you going in circles. Work the rows of medallions and link them together as you go to create this triangular masterpiece.

SIZES
Instructions are written for one size.

FINISHED MEASUREMENTS
■ Approx 51"/129.5cm wide x 25"/63.6cm long

MATERIALS
■ 8 1¾oz/50g balls (each approx 88yd/80m) of Nashua Handknits/Westminster Fibers, Inc. *Wooly Stripes* (wool) in #1 viva! ④

■ Size I/9 (5.5mm) crochet hook *or size to obtain gauge*

GAUGE
One circle is approx 3"/7.5mm measured through the diameter using size I/9 (5.5mm) crochet hook.
Take time to check gauge.

SPECIAL TECHNIQUE
Linking double crochet (ldc) used to join two circles: *Insert hook in next st in circle A, yo and pull through, insert hook in next st of circle B, yo and pull through (3 loops on hook), (yo, pull through 2 loops) 2 times. Insert hook in next st of circle A, yo and pull through, insert hook in same st of circle B, yo and pull through (3 loops on hook), (yo, pull through 2 loops) 2 times. Rep from * once more (4 ldc).

Notes
1 Shawl is worked in rows of circles that are linked together as you work each row.
2 There will be 9 rows: Row 1—17 circles, row 2—15 circles, row 3—13 circles, row 4—11 circles, row 5—9 circles, row 6—7 circles, row 7—5 circles, row 8—3 circles, row 9—1 circle.
3 Work the circle in the middle of the row first, then work the circles on each side.
4 Work with 2 or 3 skeins of yarn for each row. Use the yarn from both the outside and the inside of the skeins. This will prevent any color "pooling," and will keep the circle colors random.
5 After the rows of circles are worked, and before joining the rows, block them with a light spray of cold water and flatten them out.

FIRST ROW OF CIRCLES
Center circle (A)
Rnd 1 (RS) Ch 3, work 11 dc in 3rd ch from hook, join rnd with a sl st in top of skipped ch-2 (counts as 1 dc)—12 dc. Ch 3, do not turn.
Rnd 2 Dc in same st as joining, 2 dc in each dc around, join rnd with a sl st in top of ch-3—24 dc. Fasten off.
Circle B
Rnd 1 (RS) Ch 3, work 11 dc in 3rd ch from hook, join rnd with a sl st in top of

skipped ch-2 (counts as a dc)—12 dc. Ch 3, do not turn.

Rnd 2 Dc in same st as joining, 2 dc in next dc. Place circle A in back of circle B, WS facing each other. Count 4 dc from final join on circle A, and work 1 dc pat in next 4 dc of circle A and next 2 dc of circle B to join 2 circles. Continue around circle B, working 2 dc in each dc, join rnd with a sl st in top of ch-3. Fasten off. Continue working circles, and attaching them to the ends of other circles in this manner, until you have 8 circles on each side of circle A.

SECOND ROW OF CIRCLES

Rep instructions for row 1, with 7 circles on each side of circle A.

THIRD—NINTH ROWS OF CIRCLES

Rep instructions for row 1, with 6 (5, 4, 3, 2, 1, 0) circles on each side of circle A.

FINISHING

Joining row 2 to row 1

Note Place row 2 below row 1 so that the circles are lined up and middle 4 sts on top of circles of row 2 and middle 4 sts on bottom of circles of row 1 are adjacent. You will be joining these 4 sts in top circle to 4 sts in circle below it and working a sc in each st to the next place to join as foll:

With row 2 below row 1, join yarn and sc through 4 sts on 2nd circle from right on row 1 and first circle on right on row 2, sc in next 2 dc of same circle on row 2, sc in next 2 dc in next circle of row 2, work a sc in next 4 dc of this circle and matching circle on row 1. Rep this until last circle of row 2. Fasten off.

Join other rows in this manner. Weave in all ends.

Assembly Diagram

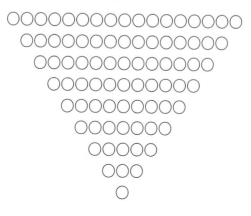

■■□▭

Lavishly loopy and fashionably furry, Marty Miller's cozy shawl features an elongated loop stitch pattern, complemented nicely by Berroco's *Chinchilla* yarn.

SIZES
Instructions are written for one size.

FINISHED MEASUREMENTS
■ Approx 63"/160cm wide x 22"/56cm long

MATERIALS
■ 18 1¾oz/50g balls (each approx 77yd/70m) of Berroco, Inc. *Chinchilla* (rayon) in #5567 olive pesto ⑤
■ Size K/10½ (6.5mm) crochet hook *or size to obtain gauge*

GAUGE
9 sc to 4"/10cm using size K/10½ (6.5mm) crochet hook.
Take time to check gauge.

Notes

1 Shawl is worked from the bottom edge to the top edge.

2 There are two ways to start this shawl. You can use the foundation single crochet (fsc) method as explained in the Stitch Glossary, which combines the foundation chain and row 1. Or you can use the regular method of making a foundation chain and working row 1 into this chain.

STITCH GLOSSARY

Loop st

Insert hook through next st, catch the 2 strands of yarn that are looped around your index finger, pull through the st, drop the lps from your finger, yo and pull through all 3 lps on hook.

Note This loop st is worked with the WS of the shawl facing you. The loops form on the RS. If you crochet right-handed, your left forefinger controls the length of the loop.

Foundation single crochet (fsc) (working foundation chain and row 1 at the same time)

Ch 2, insert hook into first ch, yo, draw up a lp, ch 1 to make base ch, yo, pull through 2 lps to finish the sc, *insert hook in the ch just made, yo, draw up a lp, ch 1, yo, pull through 2 lps; rep from *.

FOUNDATION SINGLE CROCHET METHOD

Foundation and row 1 Work 142 fsc to measure approx 63"/160cm. Ch 1, turn.

Row 2 Sc in each ch across—142 sc. Ch 1, turn.

Row 3 Loop st in each sc across—142 loop sts. Ch 1, turn.

Row 4 Sc in each loop st across. Ch 1, turn. Rep rows 3 and 4 until shawl measures approx 22"/56cm, ending with a row of sc. Do not fasten off.

Side edge

Work 2 more sc in last sc to turn the corner, working along row-ends on one side sc evenly to next corner, making sure the side lies flat. Fasten off.

Join yarn in bottom corner of other side, sc evenly along row-ends making sure the side lies flat. Fasten off.

FOUNDATION CHAIN METHOD

Ch 143.

Row 1 Sc in next 2nd ch from hook and in each ch across—142 sc. Ch 1, turn.

Row 2 Sc in each sc across—142 sc. Ch 1, turn.

Row 3 Loop st in each sc across—142 loop sts. Ch 1, turn.

Row 4 Sc in each loop st across. Ch 1, turn.

Rep Rows 3 and 4 until shawl measures approx 22"/56cm, ending with a row of sc. Do not end off.

Side edge

Work 2 more sc in last sc to turn the corner, working along row-ends on one side sc evenly to next corner, making sure the side lies flat. Fasten off.

Join yarn in bottom corner of other side, sc evenly along row-ends making sure the side lies flat. Fasten off.

FINISHING

Weave in ends.

FOUR-LEAF-CLOVER SHAWL

Lucky stitches

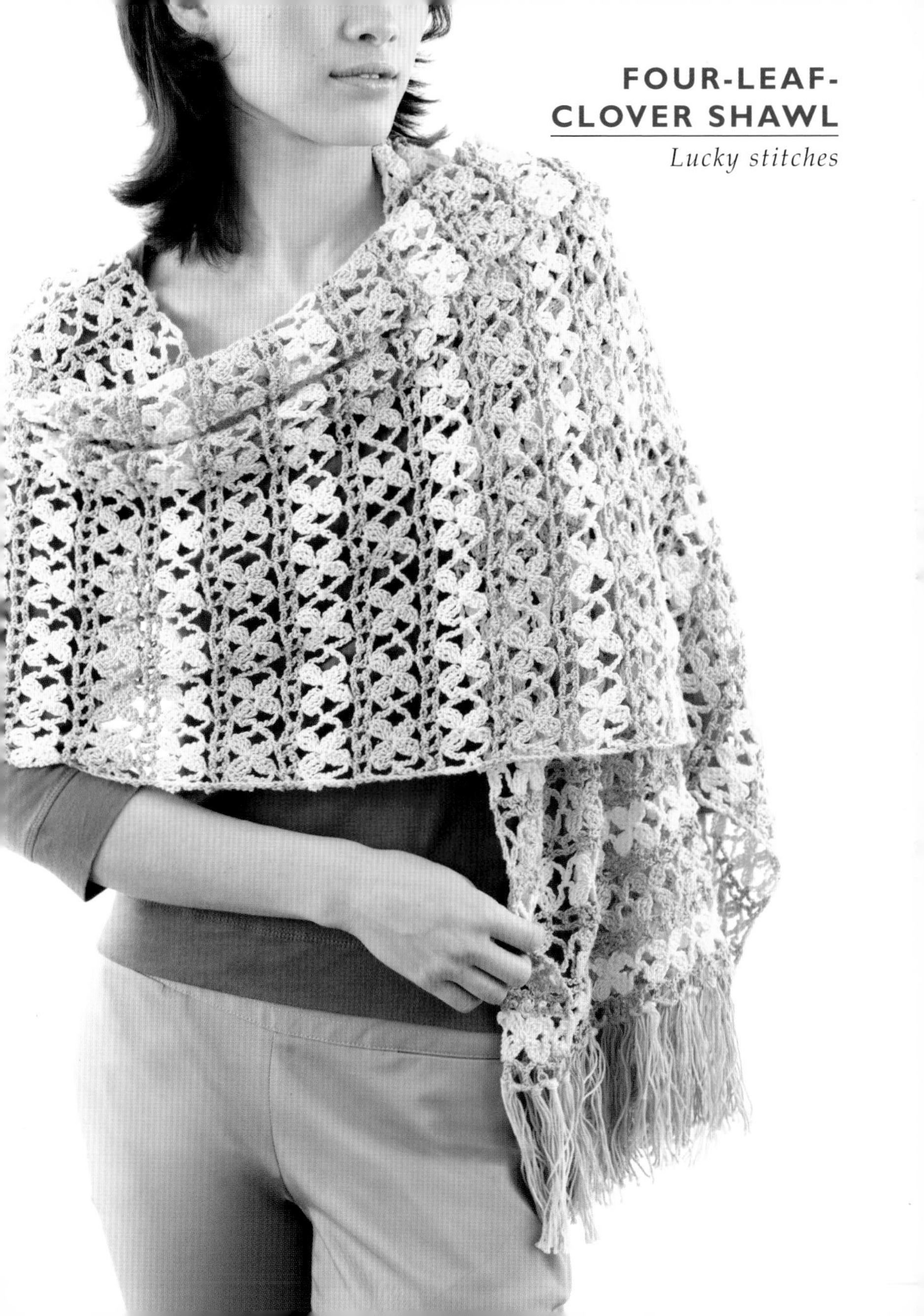

■■■▭

Created by Sasha Kagan, this shawl is a breath of fresh spring air with its alternating floral rows stitched in the palest of pastels.

SIZES
Instructions are written for one size.

FINISHED MEASUREMENTS
■ Approx 21½"/54.5cm wide x 76"/193cm long

MATERIALS
■ 3 1¾oz/50g balls (each approx 186yd/169m) of Rowan Yarns/ Westminster Fibers, Inc. *4-Ply Cotton* (cotton) in #121 ripple (A), #140 honeydew (B) and #131 fresh (C) ⓵
■ Size D/3 (3.25mm) crochet hook *or size to obtain gauge*

GAUGE
22 sts and 9 rows to 4"/10cm over flower stripe pat.
Take time to check gauge.

STITCH GLOSSARY
double treble crochet (dtr) Yo 3 times, inset hook in next st, yo, draw yarn through st, *yo, draw yarn through 2 lps on hook; rep from * 3 times.

Double treble crochet 2 together (dtr2tog) Make 2 dtr in next st until 1 lp of each rem on hook, yo and pull through all 3 lps on hook.

FLOWER STRIPE PATTERN
(multiple of 12 sts plus 11 for foundation ch)

Row 1 (RS) With A, tr in 9th ch from hook, *ch 2, sk 2 ch, tr in next ch; rep from * across. Turn.

Row 2 With B, ch 1, dc into first tr, *ch 9, sk 1 tr. (dc, ch 4, dtr2tog) in next tr, sk 1 dc, (dtr2tog, ch 4, dc) in next tr; rep from * to last 2 sps, ch 9, sk 1 tr, dc in 3rd ch. Turn.

Row 3 With B, ch 10 (counts as dtr, 4 ch), dc in first ch-9 sp, *ch 4, (dtr2tog, ch 4, sl st, ch 4, dtr2tog) in top of next dtr2tog, ch 4, dc in next ch-9 sp; rep from *, end ch 4, dtr in last dc. Turn.

Row 4 With A ch 1, dc in first dtr, *ch 5, dc in top of next dtr2tog; rep from *, end working last dc in 6th ch of ch-10 at beg of previous row. Turn.

Row 5 With A, ch 5 (count as dtr, ch 2), tr in next ch-5 sp, ch 2, tr in next dc, *ch 2, tr in next ch-5 sp, ch 2, tr in next dc, rep from * across. Turn.

Rep rows 2–5.

SHAWL
Foundation row With A, ch 155.
Follow flower stripe pat in the following color sequence:
Row 1 A
Rows 2 and 3 B
Rows 4 and 5 A
Rows 6 and 7 C
Rows 8 and 9 A

Rep rows 2–9 of stripe pat 19 times, then rep rows 2–5 once. Piece should measure approx 76"/193cm. Fasten off.

FINISHING
Block shawl loosely to measurements. Weave in ends.

FRINGE
Cut 5"/12.5cm strands of A and B. Using 3 strands of same color for each fringe, attach 50 fringes alternating 2 B fringes and 2 A fringes evenly spaced across each short end of shawl. Trim ends evenly.

Whether you re hitting the town for your morning coffee or a midnight cocktail, you ll look fabulous in this Marty Miller design. Start by working the center back in the round and finish by stitching the lacy area back and forth in rows.

SIZES

Instructions are written for one size.

FINISHED MEASUREMENTS

■ Approx 45"/114cm wide x 35"/89cm long

MATERIALS

■ 10 1¾oz/50g skeins (each approx 80yd/73m) of Crystal Palace Yarns *Deco Ribbon* (acrylic/rayon) in #9538 tulips **(5)**

■ Size K/10½ (6.5mm) crochet hook *or size to obtain gauge*

■ Small and large stitch markers

GAUGE

First 17 rnds, measured edge-to-edge across center, equal approx 9½"/24cm. *Take time to check gauge.*

STITCH GLOSSARY

sc2tog [Insert hook into next st and draw up a lp] twice, yo and draw through all 3 lps on hook.

Notes

I The center back (solid area), which is worked in-the-round, is worked first. Do not join these rnds. Place a marker at end of first rnd and move it as you work each rnd.

2 When working in rnds you will be working on the right side of the shawl. On the lacy part of the shawl you will be working back and forth in rows.

3 Shawl can be made larger by working more rows or smaller by working fewer rows, which will make the yarn requirements different.

4 When working in rows, place markers where increases occur. Place larger markers at ends of rows to indicate where to turn.

SHAWL

Center back (solid area)

Ch 4, join rnd with a sl st to form a ring.

Rnd I Ch 1, 8 sc in ring. Place marker at beg of rnd.

Rnd 2 *Sc in each of next 2 sc, ch 2; rep from * around—8 sc, 4 ch-2 sps.

Rnd 3 *Sc in each of next 2 sc, 2 sc in ch-2 sp, ch 2; rep from * around—16 sc, 4 ch-2 sps.

Rnd 4 *Sc in each of next 4 sc, 2 sc in ch-2 sp, ch 3; rep from * around—24 sc, 4 ch-3 sps.

Rnd 5 *Sc in each of next 6 sc, 2 sc in ch-3 sp, ch 3; rep from * around—32 sc, 4 ch-3 sps.

Rnd 6 *Sc in each of next 8 sc, 2 sc in ch-3 sp, ch 4; rep from * around—40 sc, 4 ch-4 sps.

Rnd 7 *Sc in each of next 10 sc, 2 sc in ch-4 sp, ch 4; rep from * around—48 sc, 4 ch-4 sps.

Rnd 8 *Sc in each of next 12 sc, 2 sc in ch-4 sp, ch 4; rep from * around—56 sc, 4 ch-4 sps.

Rnd 9 *Sc in each of next 14 sc, 2 sc in ch-4 sp, ch 5; rep from * around—64 sc, 4 ch-4 sps.

Rnd 10 *Sk 1 sc, sc in each of next 14 sc, ch 5, sc in ch-5 sp of previous rnd, ch 5; rep from * around.

Rnd 11 *Sk 1 sc, sc in each of next 12 sc, ch 5, (sc in ch-5 sp of previous rnd, ch 5) 2 times; rep from * around.

Rnd 12 *Sk 1 sc, sc in each of next 10 sc, ch 5, (sc in ch-5 sp of previous rnd, ch 5) 3 times; rep from * around.

Rnd 13 *Sk 1 sc, sc in each of next 8 sc, ch 5, (sc in ch-5 sp of previous rnd, ch 5) 4 times; rep from * around.

Rnd 14 *Sk 1 sc, sc in each of next 6 sc, ch 5, (sc in ch-5 sp of previous rnd, ch 5) 5 times; rep from * around.

Rnd 15 *Sk 1 sc, sc in each of next 4 sc, ch 5, (sc in ch-5 sp of previous rnd, ch 5) 6 times; rep from * around.

Rnd 16 *Sk 1 sc, sc in each of next 2 sc, ch 5, (sc in ch-5 sp of previous rnd, ch 5) 7 times; rep from * around.

Rnd 17 *Sc2tog, ch 5, (sc in ch-5 sp of previous rnd, ch 5) 8 times; rep from * around.

Rnd 18 *Sc in next ch-5 sp, place marker in ch-5 sp just made, (ch 5, sc in next ch-5 sp) 8 times; rep from * around. Fasten off. Place marker in last sc.

Lacy section

Row 19 Sk ch-5 sp, join yarn in next ch-5 sp, *ch 5, sc in next ch-5 sp; rep from * to next marker, ch 5, (sc in marked ch-5 sp, ch 5) 2 times; rep from *, working an inc in each marked ch-5 sp until you reach the 4th sp before marked sc, end (ch 2, dc) in sp. Turn.

Row 20 *Ch 5, sc in next ch-5 sp; rep from * to next marker, ch 5, (sc in marked ch-5 sp, ch 5) 2 times, (sc in next ch-5 sp, ch 5) 4 times, (sc in next ch-5 p, ch 5, sc in same ch-5 sp, ch 5), place marker; rep from * 2 more times, end ch 2, dc in last ch sp. Turn.

Row 21 *Ch 5, sc in next ch-5 sp; rep from * to next marker, ch 5, (sc in marked ch-5 sp, ch 5) 2 times; rep from *, end ch 2, dc in last ch-5 sp. Turn.

Row 22 Ch 5, sc in first ch-sp, *(ch 5, sc in next ch-5 sp); rep from * to next marker, ch 5, (sc in marked ch-5 sp, ch 5) 2 times; rep from * to next marker foll pat across, end ch 5, sc in last ch-sp, dc in same ch-sp. Turn.

Rows 23–44 Rep rows 21 and 22, 11 more times.

Fasten off.

Block shawl lightly to measurements. Weave in ends.

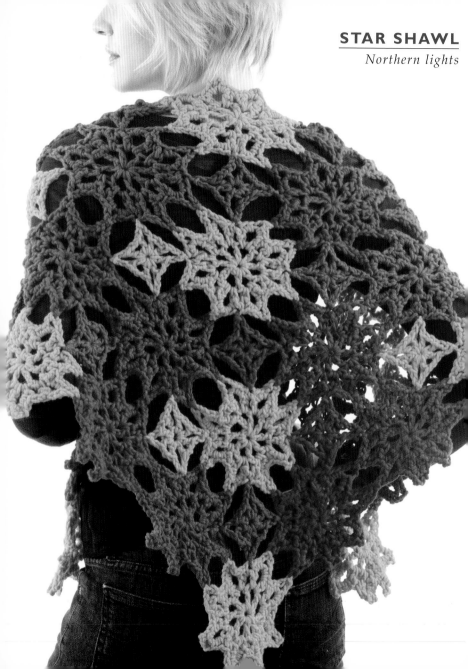

This striking design by **Annette Petavy** features alternating large motifs and joining motifs and is finished with an upper border. Grab a good book and put some logs on the fire; this delectable shawl will keep you nice and cozy.

SIZES
Instructions are written for one size.

FINISHED MEASUREMENTS
■ Approx 54"/137cm at straight edge along top of triangle and 28½"/72cm at center depth of triangle

MATERIALS
■ 3 1¾oz/50g balls (each approx 75yd/69m) of Classic Elite Yarns *Duchess* (wool/rayon/cashmere/angora/nylon) in #1089 pink damask (A) **5**
■ 3 balls in #1055 patrician port (B)
■ 2 balls in #1032 majesty's magenta (C)
■ Size L/11 (8mm) crochet hook *or size to obtain gauge*

GAUGE
One large motif is 7"/18cm across after blocking using size L/11 (8mm) crochet hook.
Take time to check gauge.

FIRST LARGE MOTIF
With A, ch 4. Join with a sl st in the 1st ch.
Round 1 Ch 5. *1 dc into ring, ch 2* Repeat from * to * 7 times. Sl st in 3rd ch at beg of round.

Round 2 Sl st in ch space. Ch 1. 1 sc in ch space. *Ch 5. 1 sc in same ch space. Ch 3. 1 sc in next ch space* Repeat from * to * 6 times. Ch 5. 1 sc in same ch space. Ch 3. 1 sl st in sc at beg of round.

Round 3 1 sl st in ch space. Ch 1. 2 sc in ch sp. *5 ch, 2 sc in same ch space, 1 sc in next —smaller—ch space, 2 sc in next—larger— ch space*. Repeat from * to * 6 times. Ch 5. 2 sc in same ch space. 1 sc in next—smaller—ch space. 1 sl st in 1st sc at beg of round. Fasten off.

FOLLOWING LARGE MOTIFS
Note Refer to diagram for colors and placement.
Rnds 1 and 2 Rep rnds 1 and 2 of first large motif.
Rnd 3 Sl st in first ch sp, ch 1 , 2 sc in next ch-5 sp, *ch 2, 1 sl st in center ch in point of motif to be joined, ch 2, 2 sc in same as last ch-5 sp, 1 sc in next ch-3 sp, 2 sc in next ch-5 sp; rep from * as many times as required for joining referring to diagram, then work any rem points as in first large motif, end 1 sl st in first sc at beg of rnd. Fasten off.

Joining motifs
Note Refer to diagram for colors and placement.
Ch 4, join with a sl st in first ch.
Rnd 1 Ch 5, *1 dc into ring, ch 2, sl st in center st between points of larger motif to be joined, ch 2, 1 dc into ring, ch 2;. rep

from * twice, 1 dc in ring, ch 2, sl st in center st between points of larger motif to be joined, ch 2, sl st in 3rd ch at beg of rnd. Fasten off.

FINISHING

Finish upper border of the shawl with ch sts, linking the motifs as follows (refer to diagram for colors and placement):

Attach the yarn with a sl st in center st of point of larger motif, ch 3, sl st in center st of point of joining motif, ch 3, sl st in center st of point of next larger motif. Fasten off. Rep from * to * 5 times to complete upper border.

Weave in all ends.

Block shawl to measurements.

Assembly Diagram

SPIRALED FLOWER SHAWL

Playful pinwheels

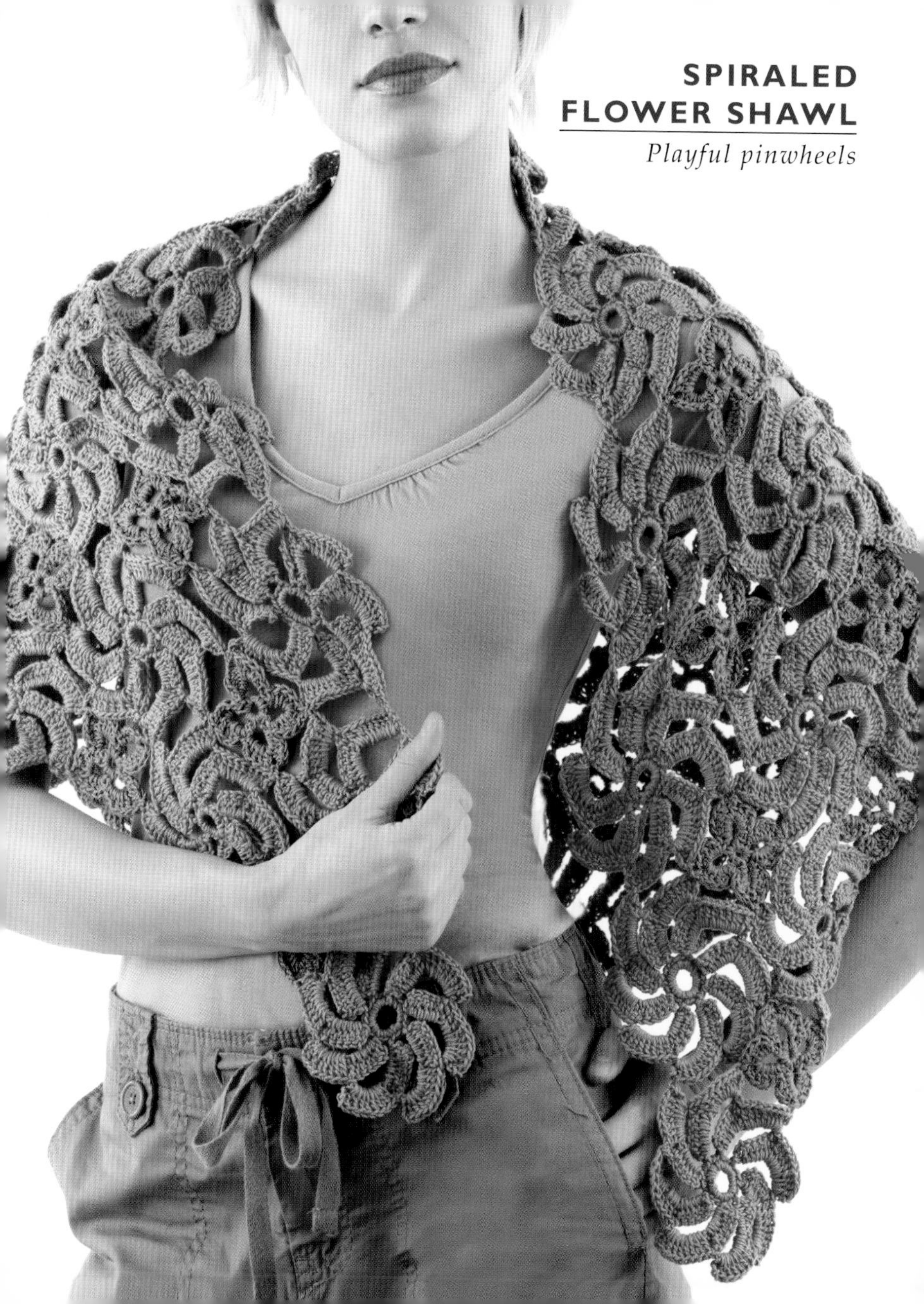

dc form the straight edge of the petal. Then sl st to the opposite end and dc back to the straight edge to form the rounded top of the petal.

![Difficulty icon]

Perfect for those chilly summer nights, this triangular shawl by Robyn Chachula features spiral flower motifs and four-point leaf motifs that are sewn together to create a lovely design.

SIZES
Instructions are written for one size.

FINISHED MEASUREMENTS
■ Approx 53"/134.5cm wide x 27"/68.5cm long

MATERIALS
■ 6 1¾oz/50g balls (each approx 123yd/112m) of Reynolds/JCA, Inc. *Saucy Sport* (cotton) in #247 sky (A) ![3]
■ 2 balls in #63 lime (B)
■ Yarn needle
■ Size G/6 (4.25 mm) crochet hook *or size to obtain gauge*

GAUGE
Spiral flower motif is 4½"/11cm in diameter.
Four point leaf motif is 2"/5cm x 2"/5cm.
Take time to check gauge.

Notes
I The flower motif is one long round. Work each petal completely before continuing to the next petal.
2 The petals of the flowers are made in 2 parts to get a rounded edge. The first set of

SPIRAL FLOWER MOTIF
(make 42)
Ch 8, join with a sl st, forming a ring. Ch 1.
Rnd I Ch 1, work 16 sc in ring, join rnd with a sl st in first sc, do not turn.
Petal I Ch 15, sl st in next sc, ch 3, turn, 5 dc in ch-15 sp, ch 3, sl st in 4th ch from ring, sl sr in next 5 ch, ch 3, turn, 8 dc in ch-15 sp, sl st to top of ch-3, do not turn.
Petal 2 Ch 9, sk next sc, sl st in next sc, ch 3, turn, 5 dc in ch-9 sp, ch 3, sl in 4th ch from ring, sl in next 5 ch, ch 3, turn, 8 dc in ch-9 sp, sl to top of ch-3, do not turn.
Petals 3–8 Rep petal 2, sl st to first petal.
Fasten off.
Weave in ends.

FOUR-POINT LEAF MOTIF
(make 36)
Ch 5, join with sl st, forming ring.
Rnd I Ch 1, [sc in ring, ch 7, sc in ring] 4 times, sl st to first sc, do not turn.
Rnd 2 (Sc, 4 dc, ch 3, 4 dc, sc) in each ch-7 sp around, sl st to first sc. Fasten off.
Leave long tail for joining.

FINISHING
Foll schematic, sew motifs tog at points on leaf motifs.

Spiral Flower Motif

Four-Point Leaf Motif

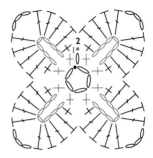

- ⬯ chain
- • slip stitch
- + single crochet
- ⊤ double crochet

Assembly Diagram

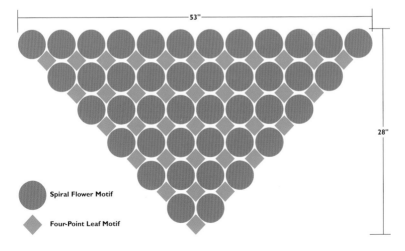

53"

28"

● Spiral Flower Motif

◆ Four-Point Leaf Motif

Jeannie Chin indulges your flair for the dramatic with her reversible rectangular lace shawl. Worked in a cotton and viscose yarn with a double chain edging, this design is just as timeless as that little black dress.

SIZES
Instructions are written for one size.

FINISHED MEASUREMENTS
■ Approx 70"/177.5cm wide x 23"/58.5cm long

MATERIALS
■ 10 1¾oz/50g balls (each approx 121yd/111m) of Filatura Di Crosa/ Tahki·Stacy Charles, Inc. *Brilla* (viscose/cotton) in #311 black ④
■ Size H/8 (5mm) crochet hook *or size to obtain gauge*

GAUGE
19½ sts and 7½ rows to 4"/10cm over crochet pat using H/8 (5.0mm) crochet hook. *Take time to check gauge.*

STITCH GLOSSARY
3-dc bobble [Yo and draw up lp, yo and draw through 2 lps] 3 times in next st, yo and draw through all 4 lps on hook.

SHAWL
Ch 338.
Row I Sc in 11th ch from hook, ch 4, sk 2 ch, dc in ch, ch 2, sk 2 ch, 3-dc bobble in next ch, ch 2, sk 2 ch, dc in ch, *ch 4, sk 2 ch, sc in next ch, ch 4, sk 2 ch, dc in ch, ch 2, sk 2 ch, 3-dc bobble in ch, ch 2, sk 2 ch, dc in ch; rep from * to last 6 ch, ch 4, sk 2 ch, sc in ch, ch 4, sk 2 ch, dc in last ch. Turn.

Row 2 Ch 11, *3-dc bobble in dc, ch 2, dc in bobble, ch 2, 3-dc bobble in dc, ch 8; rep from *, end dc in 5th ch from sc. Turn.

Row 3 Ch 5, sc in ch-8 sp, ch 2, dc in bobble, ch 2, 3-dc bobble in dc, ch 2, dc in bobble, *ch 2, sc in ch-8 sp, ch 2, dc in bobble, ch 2, 3-dc bobble in dc, ch 2, dc in bobble; rep from *, end ch 2, sc in ch-8 sp, ch 2, dc in 3rd ch of ch-11. Turn.

Row 4 Ch 5, 3-dc bobble in sc, ch 2, *dc in dc, ch 4, sc in bobble, ch 4, dc in dc, ch 2, 3-dc bobble in sc, ch 2; rep from *, end dc in 3rd ch of ch-5. Turn.

Row 5 Ch 5, dc in bobble, ch 2, 3-dc bobble in dc, ch 8, 3-dc bobble in dc, *ch 2, dc in bobble, ch 2, 3-dc bobble in dc, ch 8, 3-dc bobble in dc; rep from *, end ch 2, dc in bobble, ch 2, dc in 3rd ch of ch-5. Turn.

Row 6 Ch 5, 3-dc bobble in dc over bobble, ch 2, *dc in bobble, ch 2, sc in ch-8 sp, ch 2, dc in bobble, ch 2, 3-dc bobble in dc, ch 2; rep from *, end dc in 3rd ch of ch-5. Turn.

Row 7 Ch 7, sc in bobble, ch 4, dc in dc, ch 2, 3-dc bobble in sc, ch 2, dc in dc, *ch 4, sc in bobble, ch 4, dc in dc, ch 2, 3-dc bobble in sc, ch 2, dc in dc; rep from *, end ch 4, sc in bobble, ch 4, dc in 3rd ch of ch-5. Turn.

Row 8 Ch 11, *3-dc bobble in dc, ch 2, dc in bobble, ch 2, 3-dc bobble in dc, ch 8; rep from * end dc in 3rd ch of ch-7. Turn.

Row 9 Ch 5, sc in ch-8 sp, ch 2, dc in bobble, ch 2, 3-dc bobble in dc, ch 2, dc in bobble, *ch 2, sc in ch-8 sp, ch 2, dc in bobble, ch 2, 3-dc bobble in dc, ch 2, dc in bobble; rep from *, end ch 2, sc in ch-11 sp, ch 2, dc in 3rd ch of ch-11. Turn.

Rows 10–39 Rep rows 4–9.

Rows 40–42 Rep rows 4–6. Do not fasten off. Turn to work in the rnd.

DOUBLE CHAIN EDGING

First side

Rnd 1 Ch 1 (counts as 1 sc), sc in same ch-1 st, sc in ch-sp, *(sc in next st, 2 sc in ch-sp) to corner, sc in next st, (sc in ch-sp, 2 sc in middle ch (3rd ch) st, sc in ch-sp on side) —for corner; rep from *, end last rep with [sc in next st, 2 sc in ch-sp] to corner, sc in next st, sc in ch-sp, join rnd with a sl st to beg ch-1. Do not fasten off. Turn to work in rows along side edge.

Rnd 2 Ch 1, sl st in same st as ch-1, *ch 6, sl st in next sc, sk 1 sc, sl st in next sc; rep from * to corner, end sl st in 1st sc of corner sc. Turn.

Rnd 3 Ch 1, sl st in next sl st, *ch 8, sl st in skipped sc of row 2; rep from *, end sl st in sl st of row 2, sl st in sc of rnd 1. Fasten off.

Second side

Attach yarn to 1st sc of corner sc. Rep rows 2 and 3 for 1st side.

FINISHING

Block shawl lightly to measurements. Weave in ends.

LINKED SHAWL
Chain reaction

Designed by Suzanne Atkinson, this teal stunner is made by working crocheted rings and linking them together as you go. Finish up by stitching the border and crocheting the strips together, and *voilà* —you've got a fabulous addition to your wardrobe.

SIZES

Instructions are written for one size.

FINISHED MEASUREMENTS

■ Approx 22"/56cm wide x 74"/188cm long

MATERIALS

■ 9 1¾oz/50g balls (each approx 184yd/168m) of Brown Sheep Company *Nature Spun* (wool) in #103 deep sea ③
■ Size G/6 (4.0mm) crochet hook *or size to obtain gauge*

GAUGE

One ring is 2½"/7cm across.
Take time to check gauge.

Note

Crocheted rings are made and linked together as the work progresses. Then a border is worked on each side of the strip of rings and strips are crocheted together.

RING STRIP

(stripes A, B, C and D)

First ring

Ch 24, join rnd with a sl st to form a ring.

Rnd I Ch 3 (counts as 1 dc), 16 dc in ring, ch 1, 7 dc in ring, ch 1, 17 dc in ring, ch 1, 7 dc in ring, ch 1, join rnd with a sl st in top of ch-3—48 dc and 4 ch-1 sps. Fasten off.

Remaining linked rings

Ch 24. Sl end of ch through center of previous ring from front to back and join with a sl st.

Rnd I Work as for 1st ring rnd 1. Fasten off. Continue as established until 48 linked rings have been worked.

STRIP A

Border

Row I With RS facing, join yarn with a sl st in first ch-1 sp of first ring. Ch 7, sk 3 dc, dc in next st, ch 3, sk 3 dc, holding next ring tog with first ring, work tr through first ch-1 sp of next ring and ch-1 sp of first ring, *ch 3, sk 3 dc, dc in next st, ch 3, sk 3 dc, ch 3, work tr through first ch-1 sp of next ring and ch-1 sp of previous ring, rep from *, end ch 3, sk 3 dc, dc in next st, ch 3, sk 3 dc, tr in ch-1 sp. Fasten off.

Row 2 With RS facing, join yarn with a sl st in 4th ch of beg ch-7 of row 1. Ch 3 (counts as 1 dc), 2 dc in first ch-sp, *dc in next dc, 3 dc in next ch-3 sp, dc in next tr, 3 dc in next ch-3 sp; rep from * across. Fasten off.

Row 3 With RS facing, join yarn with a sl st in top of beg ch-3. Ch 6 (counts as sc, ch 5), *sk 3 dc, sc in next dc, ch 5, rep from *, end sc in last dc. Fasten off.

Rep border rows 1, 2 and 3 on other side of strip A.

STRIPS B, C AND D

Work border as for strip A, omitting row 3 on one side of border.

Joining strips

Row 3 Arrange strip A and strip B side by side lengthwise, row 3 of strip A to row 2 of strip B. With RS facing, join yarn with a sl st in top of ch-3 of row 2 of strip B, *ch 2, sc in next ch-5 sp of strip A, sk 3 dc in strip B, ch 2, sc in next dc of strip B; rep from * across, end ch 2, sc in last dc of strip B. Fasten off.

Join strip B to strip C as for strip A and strip B.

Join strip C to strip D as for strip A and strip B.

FINISHING

Block shawl lightly to measurements. Weave in ends.

SNOWFLAKE SHAWL

Winter rose

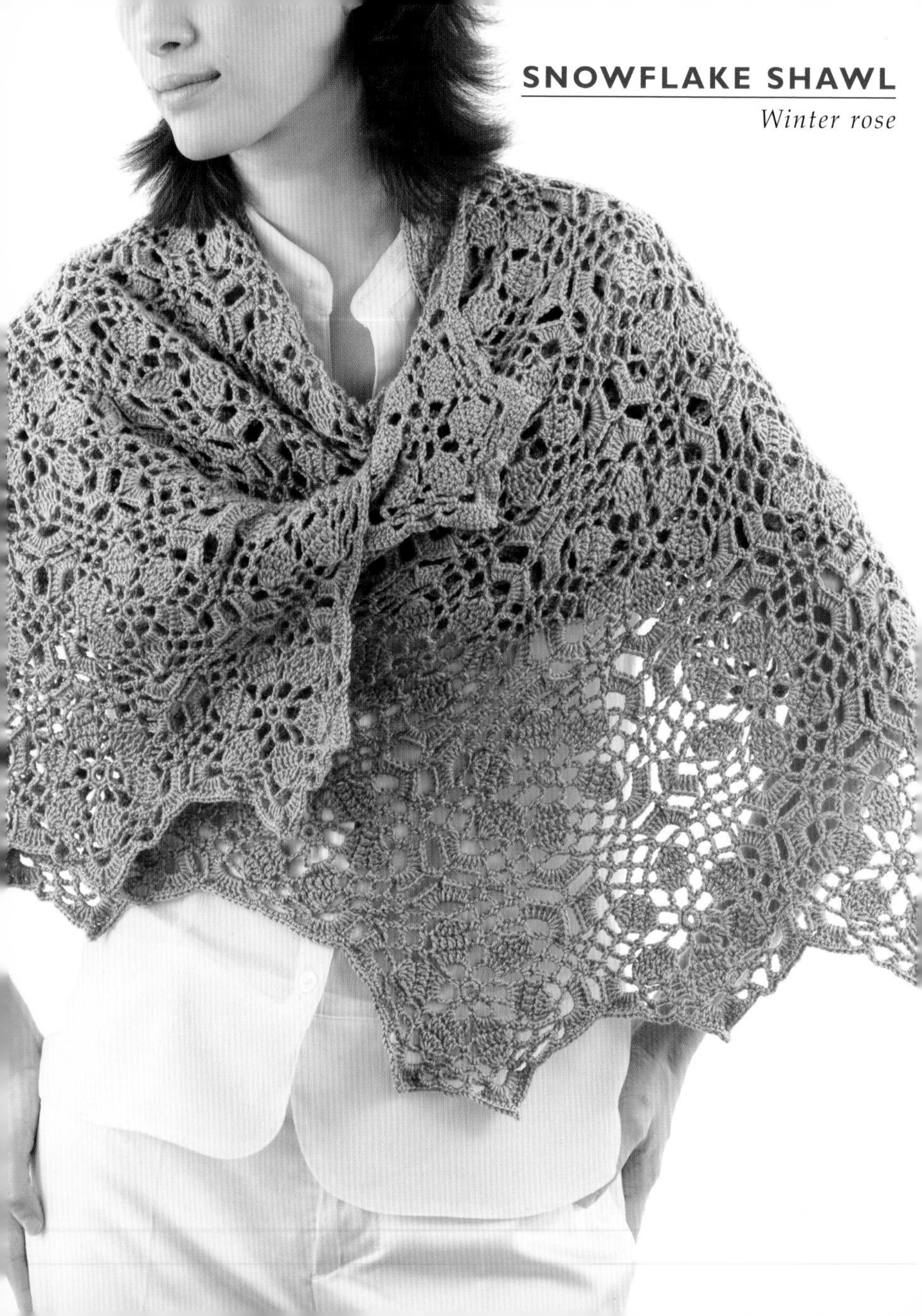

Any winter day can become a wonderland when you're wrapped in this ethereal shawl by Suzanne Atkinson. Prim and pretty, the hexagonal motifs are worked in a luscious merino, silk and wool blend.

SIZES
Instructions are written for one size.

FINISHED MEASUREMENTS
■ Approx 25"/63.5cm wide x 74"/188cm long

MATERIALS
■ 19 ⅞oz/25g balls (each approx 93yd/85m) of GGH/Muench Yarns, Inc. *Tajmahal* (wool/silk/cashmere) in #7 mauve (**2**)

■ Size G/6 (4.25mm) crochet hook *or size to obtain gauge*

GAUGE
Motif A is 5½"/14cm at widest point using size G/6 (4.25mm) crochet hook (after blocking).
Take time to check gauge.

STITCH GLOSSARY
Double crochet 4 together (dc4tog)
[Yo, insert hook into next st and draw up a lp, yo and through 2 lps on hook] 4 times, yo and draw through all 5 lps on hook.
Double crochet 5 together (dc5tog)
[Yo, insert hook into next st and draw up a lp, yo and through 2 lps on hook] 5 times, yo and draw through all 6 lps on hook.

Note
Shawl is worked in hexagonal motifs that are joined as the work progresses.

MOTIF A
Ch 6, join with a sl st to first ch forming a ring.
Rnd 1 Ch 2, 11 sc in ring, join rnd with a sl st in first ch of rnd.
Rnd 2 Ch 8 (counts as sc, ch 7), *sk 1 sc, sc in next sc, ch 7, rep from * around, end sc in next sc, sk 1 sc, ch 2, tr in 2nd ch of rnd —6 ch-7 sp.
Rnd 3 Ch 3 (counts as 1 dc), 4 dc over post of tr, *ch 3, 5 dc in ch-7 sp, rep from * around, ch 3, join rnd with a sl st in top of beg ch-3.
Rnd 4 Ch 3 (counts as 1 dc), dc in each of next 4 dc, ch 3, sc in ch-3 sp, ch 3, *dc in each of next 5 dc, ch 3, sc in ch-3 sp, ch 3, rep from * around, join rnd with a sl st in top of beg ch-3.
Rnd 5 Ch 3 (counts as 1 dc), dc4tog, *(ch 5, sc in ch-3 sp) 2 times, ch 5, dc5tog, rep from * around, (ch 5, sc in ch-3 sp) 2 times, ch 2, dc in top of dc4tog.
Rnd 6 Ch 6 (counts as sc, ch 5), *sc in ch-5 sp, ch 5, rep from * around, end sc in last ch-5 sp, ch 2, dc in first ch of rnd.
Rnd 7 Ch 4, *(5 dc, ch 3, 5 dc) in ch-5 sp, ch 3, sc in ch-5 sp, ch 5, sc in ch-5 sp, ch 3,

rep from * around, end sc, ch 5, sl st in first ch of rnd.

Fasten off.

MOTIF B

Work as for motif A through rnd 6.

Joining

Rnd 7 Ch 4, 5 dc in ch-5 sp in motif B, ch 1, sc in top right ch-3 corner of motif A, ch 1, 5 dc in same ch-5 sp of motif B, ch 1, sc in ch-5 sp of motif A, ch 1, sc in next ch-5 sp of motif B, ch 2, sc in next ch-5 sp of motif A, ch 2, sc in next ch-5 sp of motif B, ch 1, sc in next ch-5 sp of motif A, ch 1, 5 dc in next corner ch-5 sp of motif B, ch 1, sc in corner ch-3 sp of motif A, ch 1, 5 dc in same corner ch-5 sp of motif B, continue working rnd 7 as for motif A.

MOTIF C

Work as for motif B, joining motif C to motif B.

MOTIF D

Work as for motif A through rnd 6.

Joining

Rnd 7 Ch 4, 5 dc in ch-5 sp of motif D, ch 1, sc in top left corner ch-3 sp of motif A, ch 1, 5 dc in same ch-5 sp of motif D, ch 1, sc in next ch-3 sp of motif A, ch 1, sc in next ch-5 sp of motif D, ch 2, sc in next ch-5 sp of motif A, ch 2, sc in next ch-5 sp of motif D, ch 1, sc in next ch-3 sp of motif A, ch 1, 5 dc in corner ch-5 sp of motif D, ch

1, sc in corner ch-3 sp of motif A, ch 1, 5 dc in same ch-5 sp of motif D, continue working rnd 7 as for motif A.

MOTIF E

Work as for motif A through rnd 6.

Joining

Rnd 7 Ch 4, 5 dc in ch-5 sp of motif E, ch 1, sc in top right corner ch-3 sp of motif D, ch 1, 5 dc in same ch-3 sp of motif E, ch 1, sc in next ch-3 sp of motif D, ch 1, sc in next ch-5 sp of motif E, ch 2, sc in next ch-5 sp of motif D, ch 2, sc in next ch-5 sp of motif E, ch 1, sc in ch-3 sp of motif D, ch 1, 5 dc in corner ch-5 sp of motif E, ch 1, sc in joining sc, ch 1, 5 dc in same ch-5 sp of motif E, ch 1, sc in next ch-3 sp of motif A, ch 1, sc in next ch-5 sp of motif E, ch 2, sc in next ch-5 sp of motif A, ch 2, sc in next ch-5 sp of motif E, ch 1, sc in next ch-3 sp of motif A, ch 1, 5 dc in next ch-5 sp of motif E, ch 1, sc in joining sc, ch 1 5 dc in same ch-5 sp of motif E, ch 1, sc in next ch-3 sp of motif B, ch 1, sc in next ch-5 sp of motif E, ch 2, sc in next ch-5 sp of motif B, ch 2, sc in next ch-5 sp of motif E, ch 1, sc in next ch-3 sp of motif B, ch 1, 5dc in next ch-5 sp of motif E, ch 1, sc in joining sc, continue working rnd 7 as for motif A.

MOTIF F

Work as for motif A through rnd 6.

Joining

Rnd 7 Join motif F to motifs E, B and C as

for motif E, then continue working rnd 7 as for motif A.

MOTIF G
Work as for motif A through rnd 6.
Joining
Rnd 7 Join motif G to motifs F and C as for motif E, then continue working rnd 7 as for motif A.

MOTIF H
Work as for motif A through rnd 6.
Joining
Rnd 7 Join to motif D as for joining of motif D to motif A.

MOTIFS I, J, K AND L
Work and join 4 more motifs in this row. Following diagram, continuing working and joining motifs together, alternating rows of 4 and 5 motifs, finishing with a row of 5, then 4, then 3 for a total of 73 motifs.

FINISHING
Edging
Join with sl st in bottom left ch-3 corner sp of motif A, (sc, ch 3, sc) in same sp, *sc in next 5 dc, 3 sc in ch-3 sp, sk next sc, 5 sc in ch-5 sp, sk next sc, 3 sc in ch-3 sp, sc in next 5 dc, (sc, ch 3, sc) in next ch-3 corner sp, sc in next 5 dc, 3 sc in ch-3 sp, sk next sc, 5 sc in ch-5 sp, sk next sc, 3 sc in ch-3 sp, sc in 5 dc, (sc in ch-1 sp) twice, sc in next 5 dc, continue as established around edge of shawl, sl st in first sc in rnd.

Weave in ends. Block shawl lightly to measurements.

Assembly Diagram

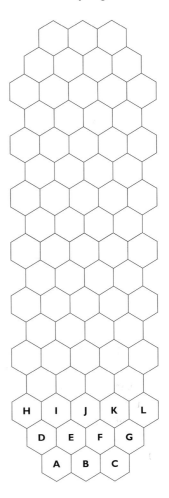

Kristen TenDyke creates an eye-catching shawl with a unique design featuring individual motifs that are joined as the work progresses.

SIZES
Instructions are written for one size.

FINISHED MEASUREMENTS
■ Approx 49"/124.5cm triangle

MATERIALS
■ 7 1¾oz/50g balls (each approx 118yd/108m) of Classic Elite Yarns *Wool Bam Boo* (wool/bamboo) in #1691 bay blue **⬛³**

■ Size F/5 (4mm) crochet hook *or size to obtain gauge*

GAUGE
One motif is 3½"/9cm triangle.
Take time to check gauge.

STITCH GLOSSARY
Back post double crochet (bpdc) Yarn over hook, starting from the front, insert hook behind, then to front around post of st in row below, yarn over and pull up a loop; (yarn over and draw through two loops on hook) twice.

FIRST MOTIF
Ch 5, join rnd with a sl st to form a ring.
Rnd 1 Ch 3, work 11 dc in ring, join rnd with a sl st in 3rd ch of beg ch-3.
Rnd 2 Insert hook behind ch-3, and work a bpdc, ch 1, *bpdc, ch 1; rep from * around, join rnd with a sl st into first bpdc.
Rnd 3 Sl st in next ch-1 sp, ch 10, sl st in 4th st from hook, ch 7, sk 1 ch-1 sp, sl st in next ch-1 sp, *ch 5, sk 1 ch-1 sp, sl st in next ch-1 sp, ch 10, sl st in 4th st from hook, ch 7, sk 1 ch-1 sp, sl st into next ch-1 sp; rep from * around, end ch 2, sk 1 ch-1 sp, dc into beg of rnd sl st. Fasten off.

JOINING MOTIF
Rep rnds 1 and 2 of 1st motif.
Rnd 3 Sl st in next ch-1 sp, ch 7, sl st in ch-3 loop at corner of joining motif, ch 7, sk 1 ch-1 sp, sl st into next ch-1 sp, **ch 2, sl st in ch-5 sp along edge of joining motif, ch 2, sk 1 ch-1 sp, sl st into next ch-1 sp, ch 7, sl st into ch-3 loop at corner of joining motif, ch 7, sk 1 ch-1 sp, sl st into next ch-1 sp; for a second joining edge rep from ** once, then finish off as for 1st motif; for an edge that is not joined, rep from * on 1st motif pat to end.

SHAWL
Note Work ends into motifs by weaving the tail over, then under, the working yarn as you work. This will save a lot of tail-weaving in the end.
Work 1st motif, then attach one edge of the next motif to one edge of the existing motif

by following the joining motif directions. Continue making and joining motifs in this manner, following chart.

FINISHING

Block piece to measurements. Weave in all rem ends.

Assembly Diagram

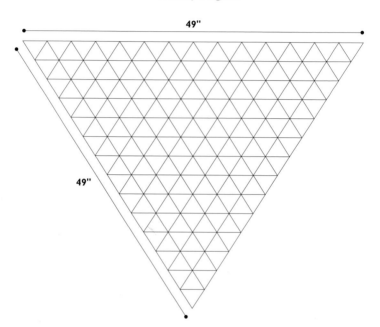

49"

49"

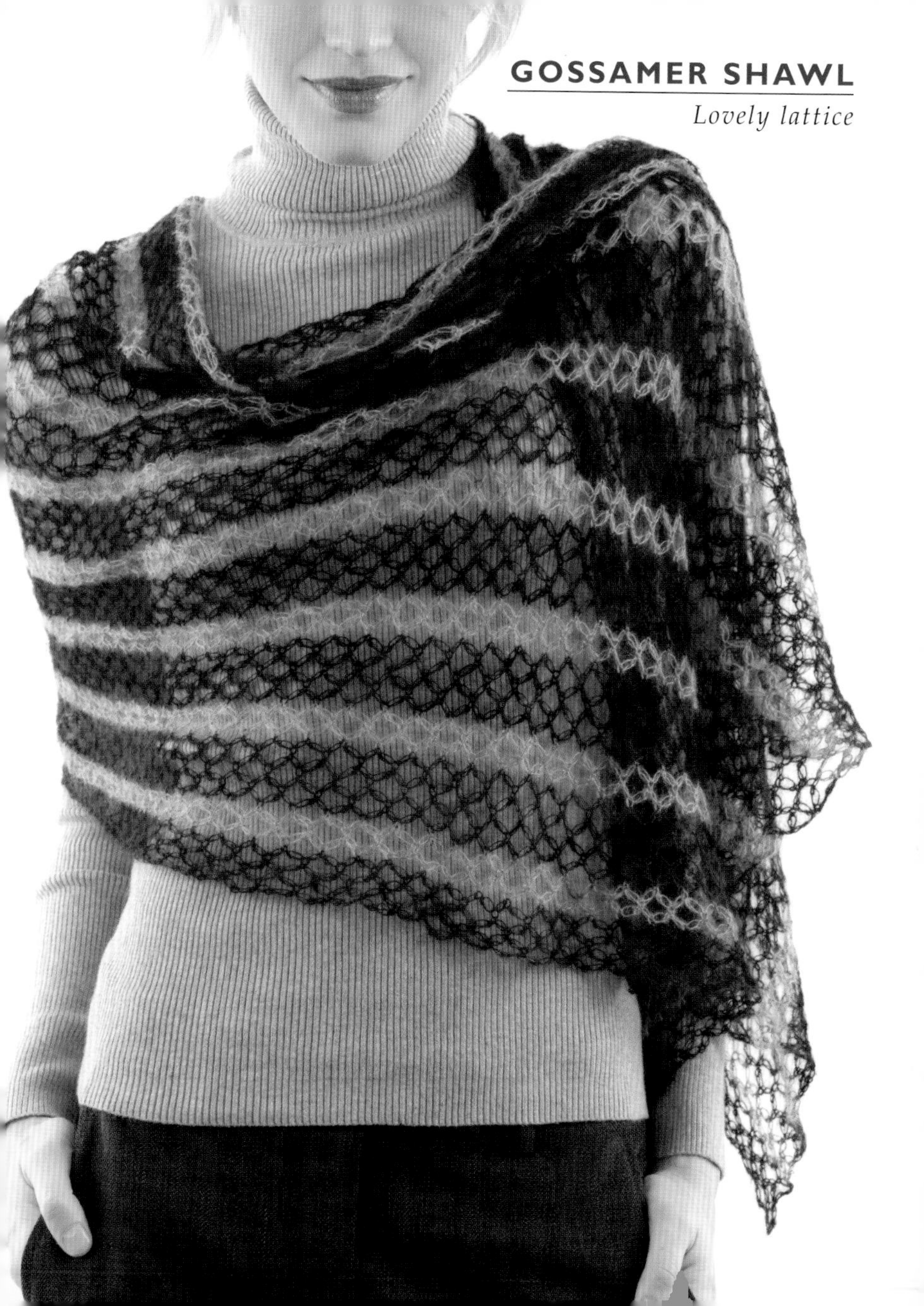

GOSSAMER SHAWL

Lovely lattice

Worked entirely in a special loop knot pattern, this Angela Juergens design is the definition of elegance. The delicate stitching and wispy mohair will transport you to a breezy balcony, with martini in hand and the Manhattan skyline in view.

SIZES

Instructions are written for one size.

FINISHED MEASUREMENTS

■ Approx 27"/68.5wide x 75"/190.5cm long

MATERIALS

■ 2 ⅞oz/25g balls (each approx 325yd/297m) of Alchemy Yarns of Transformation *Haiku* (mohair/silk) in #37e twig (A) ④

■ 1 ball in #61a winkie's blue (B)

■ Size C/2 (2.75mm) crochet hook *or size to obtain gauge*

■ Yarn needle

GAUGE

8 loop knots to 4"/10cm before blocking. *Take time to check gauge.*

SPECIAL TECHNIQUE

Note

The entire shawl is worked in a "loop knot" pattern. The loop knot is a lengthened chain stitch locked with a single crochet worked into back of loop. See illustration at right.

Loop knot pat

Make 1 chain and length the loop to ⅓". Wrap the yarn over the hook.

Draw through the loop on hook, keeping the single back thread of this long chain separate from the 2 front threads.

Insert the hook under this single back thread and wrap the yarn again.

Draw a loop through and wrap again. Draw through both loops on hook to complete.

SHAWL

For the base ch, make 163 loop knots using A.

Row 1 Work sc into sc between 3rd and 4th loops from hook, *make 2 loop knots, skip 2 loop knots from base ch, 1 sc into next sc of base ch; rep from * to end.

Row 2 Work 3 loop knots and sc into first sc after loop of previous row, *make 2 loop knots, skip 2 loop knots from previous row, 1 sc in next sc of previous row; rep from * to end.

Row 3 Work 3 loop knots and sc into first sc after loop of previous row, *make 2 loop knots, skip 2 loop knots from previous row, 1 sc in next sc of previous row; rep from * to end.

Rep rows 2 and 3 for pat throughout, working 1 more row using A, then (2 rows B, 4 rows A) 9 times. Fasten off.

FINISHING

Weave in ends and block shawl to measure 27"/68.5cm wide by 75"/190.5cm long.

Loop Knot Pattern

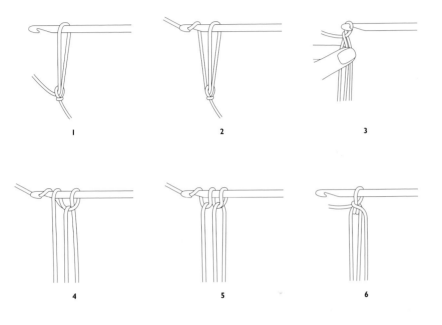

1

2

3

4

5

6

Explore your artistic side with Shiri Mor's masterful design. This shawl starts at the point and is worked in a progressive pattern of open and closed boxes.

SIZES

Instructions are written for one size.

FINISHED MEASUREMENTS

■ Approx 74"/188cm across top after blocking

MATERIALS

■ 7 1¾oz/50g balls (each approx 175yd/160m) of Koigu Wool Designs *KPPPM* (wool) in #P800 moss (A) **①**

■ 4 1¾oz/50g balls (each approx 175yd/160m) of Koigu Wool Designs *KPM* (wool) in #2236 purple (B) **①**

■ Size D/3 (3.25mm) crochet hook *or size to obtain gauge*

GAUGE

4 boxes to 3¼"/8.5cm before blocking.
4 boxes to 4"/10cm after blocking.
Take time to check gauge.

STITCH GLOSSARY

Double treble crochet (dtr) Yo 3 times, insert hook into st, yo and draw up a lp, [yo and draw through 2 lps on hook] 4 times.

First box of each row (including row 1) Ch 7, sk 4 ch, tr in each of next 3 ch.

Closed box Sc in next ch sp, ch 3, 3 tr in same ch sp.

Open box Sc in next ch sp, ch 7.

Note

Using A, follow chart for 72 rows. The 2 colors in the chart are used only to differentiate between rows. Work the entire chart using A only.

SHAWL

Using A and beg with row 1, ch 7, sk 4 ch, tr in each of next 3 ch. Continue to follow chart for 72 rows.

Top edging

Using B, work 2 more rows working closed boxes only (74 rows total, 74 boxes across top) as follows:

Row 1 *Ch 4, sc in next ch-sp; rep from * 73 more times, ch 4, sc in same sp, ch 2, turn.

Row 2 Hdc in first sc, *4 hdc in next sp, hdc in next sc; rep from * 74 more times. Fasten off.

Side edging

Foundation row Using B, work 296 hdc evenly down one side of the shawl (4 hdc per row edge), 1 hdc at bottom corner and 296 more hdc up other edge, ch 1, turn.

Row 1 Sc in first hdc, *ch 5, sk 3 hdc, sc in next hdc; rep from * to corner hdc, ch 9, sc again in corner hdc, **ch5, sk 3 hdc, sc in next hdc; rep from * to last 4 sts, sk 3 hdc, tr in last hdc, turn.

Row 2 *Ch 7, sc in next ch-sp; rep from * to center loop, ch 7, sc again in center loop, **ch 7, sc in next ch-sp; rep from ** to next to last ch-sp, ch 3, dtr in last ch-sp, turn.

Row 3 Ch 3, 3 tr in first ch-sp, work closed boxes to center loop, (sc, ch 7) in center loop, work a closed box in center loop and closed boxes across to last ch-sp, sc in last ch-sp, ch 1, turn.

Row 4 Sl st in each of first 3 tr, work closed boxes to center loop, (sc, ch 7) in center loop, work a closed box in center space and closed boxes across to next to last ch-sp, sc in last ch-sp, ch 1, turn.

Row 5 Sl st in each of first 3 tr, work open boxes to center loop, work 2 open boxes in center loop, work open boxes to next to last ch-sp, ch 3, dtr in last ch-sp, turn.

Row 6 Ch 7, work open boxes to center loop, work 2 open boxes in center loop, work open boxes to next to last ch-sp, ch 3, dtr in last ch-sp, turn.

Row 7 *Ch 4, sc in next ch-sp; rep from * to center loop, ch 4, sc again in center loop, **ch 4, sc in next ch-sp; rep from ** to end, ch 2, turn.

Row 8 Hdc in first sc, *4 hdc in next sp, hdc in next sc; rep from * to end.
Fasten off.

FINISHING

Weave in all loose ends.

To block, wet shawl in warm water and hang from top, allowing it to drape.

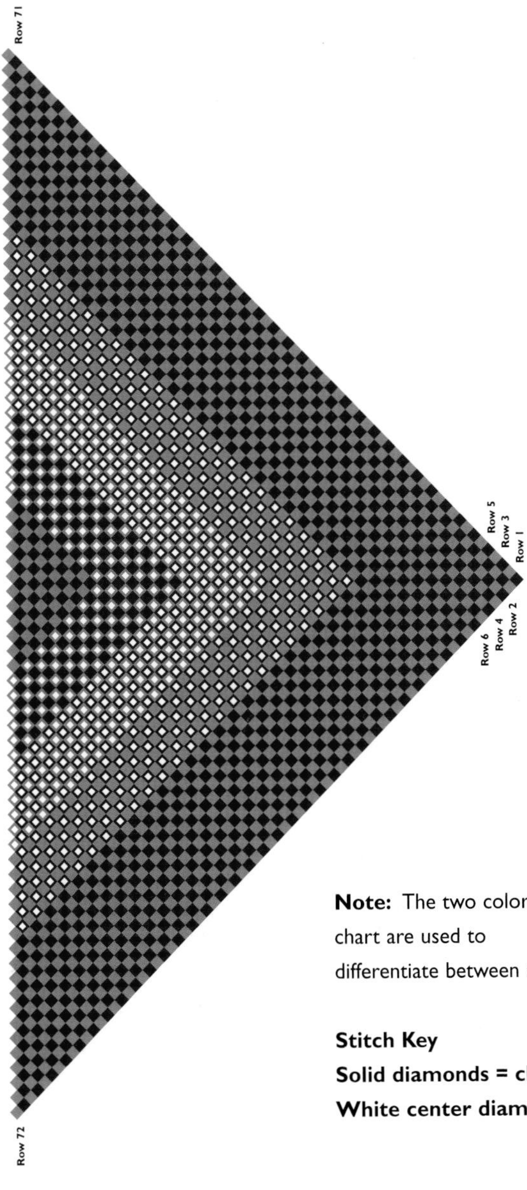

Row 71

Row 5
Row 3
Row 1

Row 6
Row 4
Row 2

Row 72

Note: The two colors on the chart are used to differentiate between rows.

Stitch Key
Solid diamonds = closed boxes
White center diamonds = open boxes

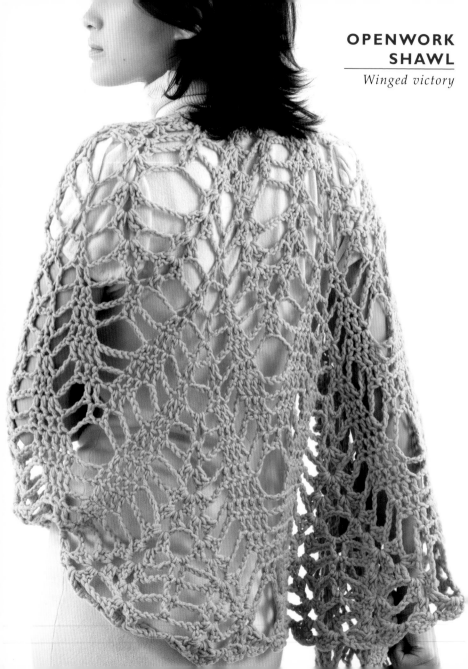

Inspired by a thread crochet doily, Doris Chan s lacy design is irresistibly cozy and surprisingly lightweight. It drapes beautifully on the body.

SIZES
Instructions are written for one size.

FINISHED MEASUREMENTS
■ Approx finished length (at back neck) 25"/63.5cm, 62"/167.5cm (at front edge)

MATERIALS
■ 7 1¾oz/50g balls (each approx 94yd/86m) of Tahki Yarns/Tahki•Stacy Charles, Inc. *Torino* (extra fine merino wool) in #213 sky blue ▨
■ Size J/10 (6 mm) crochet hook *or size to obtain gauge*

GAUGE
Approx 10 base ch/sc and 4 rows shells to 4"/10cm.
Take time to check gauge.

Notes
I Gauge is not critical; keep work relaxed for laciest effect and to achieve finished length.
2 This shawl must be blocked to open up the stitch pattern and to achieve full finished length.

STITCH GLOSSARY
Foundation single crochet (fsc) This technique creates a foundation chain and a row of sc in one for a sturdy, elastic neckline. Start with a slip knot, ch 2, insert hook in 2nd ch from hook, draw up a lp, yo and draw through one lp (the "chain"), yo and draw through 2 lps (the "sc"). The following st is worked under the forward 2 lps of the stem of the prev st (into the "chain"). Insert hook into the face of the "chain" and under the nub at the back of the "chain," draw up a lp, yo and draw through one lp (the "chain"), yo and draw through 2 lps (the "sc"). Rep for the length of foundation.
Shell [2 dc, ch 3, 2 dc] in same st or sp.
Inc-shell [2 dc, ch 3, 2 dc, ch 3, 2 dc] in same st or sp.
V [dc, ch 3, dc] in same st or sp.

SHAWL
Note Shawl is like a round doily with a wedge missing, worked back and forth in rows. The sections repeat across the row. The pattern creates its own edging.
Base ch/sc 31 to measure approx 12½"/31.5cm stretched.
Back neck edging
Ch 3, dc in first sc, [sk next 2 sc, (sl st, ch 3, dc) in next sc] 9 times, sk next 2 sc, sl st in last sc, do not turn—10 scallops.
Rotate, work across opposite side of fsc.
Row I Ch 2, shell in first ch, *ch 3, sk next ch, sc in next ch, ch 5, sc in next ch, ch 3,

sk next ch, shell in next ch*; rep from * to * 5 times, turn.

Row 2 Ch 2, *inc-shell in next ch-sp of shell, ch 3, sk next ch-sp and sc, (sc, ch 5, sc) in next ch-5 sp, ch 3, sk next sc and ch-sp*; rep from * to * 5 times, inc-shell in last ch-sp of shell, turn.

Row 3 Ch 2, *shell in next ch-sp of inc-shell, ch 1, shell in next ch-sp of inc-shell**, ch 3, sk next ch-sp and sc, (sc, ch 5, sc) in next ch-5 sp, ch 3, sk next sc and ch-sp*; rep from * to * 5 times, rep from * ending at **, turn.

Row 4 Ch 2, *shell in next ch-sp of shell, ch 5, shell in next ch-sp of shell**, ch 3, sk next ch-sp and sc, sc in next ch-5 sp, ch 3, sk next sc and ch-sp*; rep from * to * 5 times, rep from * ending at **, turn.

Row 5 Ch 2, *shell in next ch-sp of shell, ch 3, dc in next ch-5 sp, ch 3, shell in next ch-sp of shell, ch 5*; rep from * to * 6 times, except omit last ch 5, turn.

Row 6 Ch 2, *shell in next ch-sp of shell, ch 3, sk next ch-sp, V in next dc, ch 3, sk next ch-sp, shell in next ch-sp of shell, ch 3*; rep from * to * 6 times, except omit last ch 3, turn.

Row 7 Ch 2, *shell in next ch-sp of shell, [ch 3, sk next ch-sp, 2 dc in next dc of V] 2 times, ch 3, sk next ch-sp, shell in next ch-sp of shell*; rep from * to * 6 times, turn.

Row 8 Ch 2, shell in next ch-sp of shell, *ch 3, sk next ch-sp, dc in each of next 2 dc, ch 3, dc in next ch-3 sp, ch 3, dc in each of next 2 dc, ch 3**, (2 dc in next ch-sp of shell) 2 times*; rep from * to * 5 times, rep from * ending at **, sk next ch-sp, shell in last ch-sp of shell, turn.

Row 9 Ch 2, shell in next ch-sp of shell, ch 3, sk next ch-sp,* 2 dc in next dc, dc in next dc, ch 3, sk next ch-sp, V in next dc, ch 3, sk next ch-sp, dc in next dc, 2 dc in next dc**, ch 4, sk next ch-sp and dc, dc in each of next 2 dc, ch 4, sk next dc and ch-sp*; rep from * to * 5 times, rep from * ending at **, ch 3, sk next ch-sp, shell in last ch-sp of shell, turn.

Row 10 Ch 2, shell in next ch-sp of shell, *ch 3, sk next ch-sp, dc in each of next 3 dc, [ch 3, sk next ch-sp, 2 dc in next dc] 2 times, ch 3, sk next ch-sp, dc in each of next 3 dc, ch 3, sk next ch-sp**, dc in each of next 2 dc*; rep from * to * 5 times, rep from * ending at **, end with shell in last ch-sp of shell, turn.

Row 11 Ch 2, shell in next ch-sp of shell, ch 3, sk next ch-sp, *2 dc in next dc, dc in each of next 2 dc, [ch 3, sk next ch-sp, dc in each of next 2 dc] 3 times, 2 dc in next dc**, ch 5, sk next (ch-sp, 2 dc, ch-sp)*; rep from * to * 6 times, rep from * ending at **, ch 3, shell in last ch-sp of shell, turn.

Row 12 Ch 2, shell in next ch-sp of shell, *ch 3, sk next ch-sp, dc in each of next 4 dc, ch 3, sk next ch-sp, 2 dc in next dc, dc in next dc, ch 3, V in next ch-sp, ch 3, dc in next dc, 2 dc in next dc, ch 3, sk next ch-sp, dc in each of next 4 dc*; rep from * to * 6 times, ch 3, sk next ch-sp, shell in last ch-sp of shell, turn.

Row 13 Ch 2, shell in next ch-sp of shell, ch 3, *sk next ch-sp, dc in each of next 3 dc, ch 4, sk next dc and ch-sp, dc in each of next 3 dc, ch 3, sk next ch-sp, V in next ch-sp of V, ch 3, sk next ch-sp, dc in each of next 3 dc, ch 4, sk next ch-sp and dc, dc in each of next 3 dc, ch 1*; rep from * to * 6 times, except omit last ch 1, instead end with ch 3, sk next ch-sp, shell in last ch-sp of shell, turn.

Row 14 Ch 2, shell in next ch-sp of shell, ch 3, sk next ch-sp, *dc in each of next 2 dc, ch 3, sk next dc and ch-sp, 2 dc in next dc, dc in each of next 2 dc, ch 3, sk next ch-sp, shell in next ch-sp of V, ch 3, sk next ch-sp, dc in each of next 2 dc, 2 dc in next dc, ch 3, sk next ch-sp and dc, dc in each of next 2 dc, ch 1, sk next ch-1 sp*; rep from * to * 6 times, except omit last ch 1, instead end with ch 3, sk next ch-sp, shell in last ch-sp of shell, turn.

Row 15 Ch 2, inc-shell in next ch-sp of shell, ch 3, *sk next ch-sp, dc in next dc, ch 3, sk next dc and ch-sp, dc in each of next 4 dc, ch 3, sk next ch-sp, inc-shell in next ch-sp of shell, ch 3, sk next ch-sp, dc in each of next 4 dc, ch 3, sk next ch-sp and dc, dc in next dc, ch 1*; rep from * to * 6 times, except omit last ch 1, instead end with ch 3,

sk next ch-sp, inc-shell in last ch-sp of shell, turn.

Row 16 Ch 2, shell in next ch-sp of shell, ch 3, *5 dc in next ch-sp of shell, ch 4, sk next (ch-sp, dc, ch-sp), 2 dc in next dc, dc in each of next 3 dc, ch 3, sk next ch-sp, shell in each of next 2 ch-sp of inc-shell, ch 3, sk next ch-sp, dc in each of next 3 dc, 2 dc in next dc, ch 4**, sk next (ch-sp, 2 dc, ch-sp)*; rep from * to * 5 times, rep from * ending at **, sk next (ch-sp, dc, ch-sp), 5 dc in next ch-sp of inc-shell, ch 3, shell in next ch-sp of inc-shell, turn.

Row 17 Ch 2, shell in next ch-sp of shell, *[ch 3, sk next ch-sp, dc in each of next 5 dc] 2 times**, [ch 3, shell in next ch-sp of shell] 2 times*; rep from * to * 6 times, rep from * ending at **, ch 3, sk next ch-sp, shell in last ch-sp of shell, turn.

Row 18 Ch 2, shell in next ch-sp of shell, *ch 4, sk next ch-sp and dc, dc in each of next 4 dc, ch 3, sk next ch-sp, dc in each of next 4 dc, ch 4, sk next dc and ch-sp, shell in next ch-sp of shell**, ch 3, (sc, ch 5, sc) in next ch-sp, ch 3, shell in next ch-sp of shell*; rep from * to * 6 times, rep from * ending at **, turn.

Row 19 Ch 2, *inc-shell in next ch-sp of shell, ch 3, sk next ch-sp and dc, dc in each of next 3 dc, ch 1, sk next ch-sp, dc in each of next 3 dc, ch 3, sk next ch-sp, inc-shell in ch-sp of next shell**, ch 3, sk next ch-sp and sc, (sc, ch 5, sc) in next ch-5 sp, ch 3, sk next sc and ch-sp*; rep from * to * 6 times, rep from * ending at **, turn.

Row 20 Ch 2, *shell in next ch-sp of inc-shell, ch 1, shell in next ch-sp of inc-shell, ch 3, sk next ch-sp and dc, dc in each of next 2 dc, ch 1, sk next ch-sp, dc in each of next 2 dc, ch 3, sk next dc and ch-sp, shell in next ch-sp of inc-shell, ch 1, shell in next ch-sp of inc-shell**, ch 3, sk next ch-sp and sc, (sc, ch 5, sc) in next ch-5 sp, ch 3, sk next sc and ch-sp*; rep from * to * 6 times, rep from * ending at **, turn.

Row 21 Ch 2, *[shell in next ch-sp of shell, ch 3] 2 times, sk next ch-sp and dc, dc in next dc, ch 1, sk next ch-sp, dc in next dc, ch 3, sk next dc and ch-sp, [shell in next ch-sp of shell, ch 3] 2 times**, sk next ch-sp and sc, sc in next ch-5 sp, ch 3, sk next sc and ch-sp*; rep from * to * 6 times, rep from * ending at **, except omit last ch 3, turn.

Row 22 Ch 2, *[shell in next ch-sp of shell, ch 3] 2 times, sk next [ch-sp, (dc, ch-1, dc) ch-sp], [shell in next ch-sp of shell, ch 3] 2 times**, sk next (ch-sp, sc, ch-sp)*; rep from * to * 6 times, rep from * ending at **, except omit last ch 3, turn.

Row 23 Ch 3, dc in first dc, [sl st, ch 3, dc] in each ch-3 sp across, end with sl st in top of tch. Fasten off.

FINISHING

Block lightly to measurements. Weave in ends.

CIRCLES SHAWL

Mohair medallions

■■■▢

Vibrant and stylish, this Angela Juergens design is worked in different circles consisting of 1, 2, 3 or 4 rounds of double crochet that are sewn together for an innovative look.

SIZES
Instructions are written for one size.

FINISHED MEASUREMENTS
■ Approx 82"/208cm along outer edge and 12"/30.5cm wide at center back

MATERIALS
■ 2 1¾oz/50g balls (each approx 110yd/100m) of Trendsetter Yarns *Rapunzel* (mohair/wool/polyamide) each in #354 brown (B), #348 fuchsia (F) and #352 royal (R) ▨
■ 1 ball each in #52 teal (T) and #353 purple (P)
■ Size E/4 (3.5mm) crochet hook *or size to obtain gauge*
■ Yarn needle

GAUGE
1-rnd circle is approx 1½"/4cm in diameter.
2-rnd circle is approx 2½"/6.5cm in diameter.
3-rnd circle is approx 3"/7.5cm in diameter.
4-rnd circle is approx 3½"/9cm in diameter.
Take time to check gauge.

Note
Shawl is worked in different size circles consisting of 1, 2, 3 or 4 rounds of double crochet.

BASIC CIRCLE
Ch 4, join rnd with a sl st to form a ring.
Rnd 1: Ch 2 (does not count as a dc), inserting the hook into the center of base ch, work 18 dc in ring, join rnd with a sl st in beg ch-2—18 dc.
Rnd 2: Ch 2 (does not count as a dc), *2 dc in each of next 2 dc, 1 dc in next dc; rep from * 4 times more, end 2 dc in each of last 3 dc, join rnd with a sl st in beg ch-2—31 dc.
Rnd 3: Ch 2 (does not count as a dc), *2 dc in next dc, 1 dc in next dc; rep from * 14 times more, end 2 dc in last dc, join rnd with a sl st in beg ch-2—47 dc.
Rnd 4: Ch 2 (does not count as a dc), *2 dc in next dc, 1 dc in each of next 2 dc; rep from * 14 times more, end 2 dc in next dc, 1 dc in last dc, join rnd with a sl st in beg ch-2—63 dc.

SHAWL
1-rnd circles
Make 9 brown (B), 12 fuchsia (F), 6 purple (P), 8 royal (R), 9 teal (T)
2-rnd circles
Make 7 brown (B), 4 fuchsia (F), 3 purple

(P), 5 royal (R), 3 teal (T)

3-rnd circles

Make 3 brown (B), 1 fuchsia (F), 3 purple (P), 5 royal (R), 4 teal (T)

4-rnd circles

Make 1 brown (B), 2 fuchsia (F), 1 purple (P), 1 royal (R), 1 teal (T)

FINISHING

Following diagram on page 78, join the 88 circles using yarn needle and matching-color yarn.

⊃　chain

•　slip stitch

⊤　double crochet

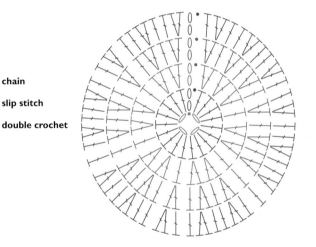

Assembly Diagram

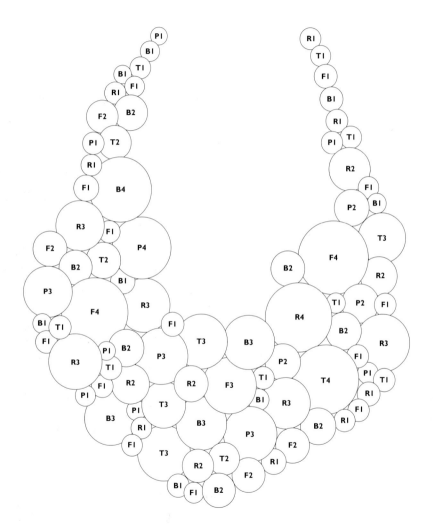

WRAP SHAWL
Sea shawl

Linda Medina alternates wide stripes of double crochet and narrow stripes of single crochet to create a lovely wrap shawl worthy of a sailor s dream. Tie the mesh ends for style that will stay put.

SIZES
Instructions are written for one size.

FINISHED MEASUREMENTS
■ Approx 14"/35.5cm wide x 86"/216cm long

MATERIALS
■ 3 4oz/113g hanks (each approx 240yd/219m) of Fiesta Yarns *Starburst La Boheme* (rayon) in alaska (A)
■ 2 2oz/57g hanks (each approx 220yd/201m) of Fiesta Yarns *La Luz* (spun silk) in bluebonnet (B)
■ Sizes G/6 (4.5mm) and J/10 (6mm) crochet hooks *or sizes to obtain gauge*

GAUGE
10 sts and 8 rows to 4"/10cm.
Take time to check gauge.

Note
Read instructions on label before winding yarn into a ball.

BODY OF SHAWL
Pattern I
With larger hook and A, ch 100 loosely.
Row I Dc in 3rd ch from hook and in each ch across—98 dc. Turn.

Rows 2—4 Ch 3 (does not count as a dc), dc in each dc across. Turn.
Change to smaller hook and B.
Row 5 Ch 1, work 3 sc in first dc, 2 sc in each dc across—197 sc. Turn.
Row 6 Ch 1, sc in each sc across. Turn.
Change to larger hook and A.
*Row 7 Ch 3 (does not count as a dc), dc in first dc, *sk next sc, dc in next sc; rep from * across—98 dc.
Rows 8—10 Rep rows 2–4.
Change to smaller hook and B.
Row I I Rep row 5.
Row I 2 Rep row 6.
Change to larger hook and A.*
Rep from rows 7–12 from * to * 2 times more.
Rep rows 7–10 once.
Fasten off.

Edging
With RS facing and larger hook, attach A with a sl st in the corner of one long side.
Row I Ch 1, sc in first dc and in each dc across.
Fasten off and weave in tail.
Rep edging on opposite long side of shawl.

MESH TIES
Pattern 2
With RS facing and smaller hook, attach B with a sl st in the corner of one short end of shawl.

Row 1 Sc in same sp as joining, ch 5, sc between Rows 1 and 2 of body, *ch 5, sc between next 2 rows of body; rep from * across—21 sc. Turn.

Row 2 *Ch 5, sc in next ch-5 sp; rep from * across—20 sc. Turn.

Rows 3—34 Rep row 2.

Note Mesh section should measure approx 17"/43cm.

Row 35 sl st in first ch-5 sp, *ch 5, sc in next ch-5 sp; rep from * to next to last ch-5 sp—18 sc. Turn.

Rows 36—41 Rep row 35—8 sc rem at end of row 41.

Fasten off.
Rep mesh tie on opposite short end of body.

Mesh edging
With RS facing and smaller hook, attach B with a sl st where B was joined to body.

Row 1 Ch 1, 3 sc in ch-5 sp, sc in next sc; rep from * around outer mesh tie edge. Fasten off and weave in tail.

FINISHING
Block shawl lightly to measurements. Weave in ends.

Assembly Diagram

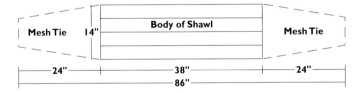

MONDRIAN
SHAWL

Simply modern

■■□▭

Sara Graham proves it's hip to be rectangular with her geometric creation. The rectangles are made separately, then edged in black and joined to create a chic, ultra-mod design.

Instructions are written for one size.

FINISHED MEASUREMENTS
■ Approx 19½"/49.5cm wide x 55"/139.5cm long

MATERIALS
■ 2 4oz/113g balls (each approx 335yd/306m) of Red Heart/Coats & Clark *Luster Sheen* (acrylic) in #7 vanilla (A)
(2)
■ 1 ball each #824 medium blue (B), #913 warm red (C), #2 black (D) and #227 buttercup (E)
■ Size F/5 (4mm) crochet hook *or size to obtain gauge*
■ Yarn needle

GAUGE
20 hdc and 16 rows to 4"/10cm.
Take time to check gauge.

RECTANGLE I
With A, ch 56.
Row I Hdc into 2nd ch from hook (counts as 1 hdc), hdc in each ch across. Ch 2, turn.
Row 2 Hdc in each hdc across. Ch 2, turn.
Rows 3–72 Rep row 2. Fasten off. Piece

should measure approx 11"/28cm x 19½"/49.5cm.

RECTANGLE 2
With B, ch 23.
Row I Hdc into 2nd ch from hook (counts as 1 hdc), hdc in each ch across. Ch 2, turn.
Row 2 Hdc in each hdc across. Ch 2, turn.
Row 3–24 Rep row 1. Fasten off. Piece should measure approx 4½"/11.5cm x 6"/15cm.

RECTANGLE 3
With A, ch 70.
Row I Hdc in 2nd ch from hook (counts as 1 hdc), hdc in each ch across. Ch 2, turn.
Row 2 Hdc in each hdc across. Ch 2, turn.
Rows 3–32 Rep row 1. Fasten off. Piece should measure approx 15"/38cm x 8½"/21.5cm.

RECTANGLE 4
With C, ch 70.
Row I Hdc in 2nd ch from hook (counts as 1 hdc), hdc in each ch across. Ch 2, turn.
Row 2 Hdc in each hdc across. Ch 2, turn.
Rows 3–14 Rep row 1. Fasten off. Piece should measure approx 15"/38 x 3½"/9cm.

RECTANGLE 5
With B, ch 60.
Row I Hdc in 2nd ch from hook (counts as 1 hdc), hdc in each ch across. Ch 2, turn.
Row 2 Hdc in each hdc across. Ch 2, turn.
Rows 3–46 Rep row 1. Fasten off. Piece

should measure approx 12"/30.5cm x 12"/30.5cm.

RECTANGLE 6

With D, ch 60.

Row 1 Hdc in 2nd ch from hook (counts as 1 hdc), hdc in each ch across. Ch 2, turn.

Row 2 Hdc in each hdc across. Ch 2, turn.

Rows 3–6 Rep row 1. Fasten off. Piece should measure approx 12"/30cm x 1½"/4cm.

RECTANGLE 7

With A, ch 104.

Row 1 Hdc into 2nd ch from hook (counts as first hdc), hdc in each ch across. Ch 2, turn.

Row 2 Hdc in each hdc across. Ch 2, turn.

Row 3–24 Rep row 1. Fasten off. Piece should measure approx 22"/56cm x 6"/15cm.

RECTANGLE 8

With D, ch 70.

Row 1 Hdc into 2nd ch from hook (counts as first hdc), hdc in each ch across. Ch 2, turn.

Row 2 Hdc in each hdc across. Ch 2, turn.

Rows 3–6 Rep row 1. Fasten off. Piece should measure approx 15"/38cm x 1½"/4cm.

RECTANGLE 9

With A, ch 48.

Row 1 Hdc into 2nd ch from hook (counts

as first hdc), hdc in each ch across. Ch 2, turn.

Row 2 Hdc in each hdc across. Ch 2, turn.

Rows 3–52 Rep row 1. Fasten off. Piece should measure approx 9½"/24cm x 12"/30.5cm.

RECTANGLE 10

With E, ch 70.

Row 1 Hdc into 2nd ch from hook (counts as first hdc), hdc in each ch across. Ch 2, turn.

Row 2 Hdc in each hdc across. Ch 2, turn.

Rows 3–24 Rep row 1. Fasten off. Piece should measure approx 15"/38cm x 6"/15cm.

RECTANGLE 11

With D, ch 6.

Row 1 Hdc into 2nd ch from hook (counts as first hdc), hdc in each ch across. Ch 2, turn.

Row 2 Hdc in each hdc across. Ch 2, turn.

Rows 3–52 Rep row 1. Fasten off. Piece should measure approx 1½"/4cm x 12"/30.5cm.

RECTANGLE 12

With E, ch 19.

Row 1 Hdc into 2nd ch from hook (counts as first hdc), hdc in each ch across. Ch 2, turn.

Row 2 Hdc in each hdc across. Ch 2, turn.

Rows 3–52 Rep row 1. Fasten off. Piece should measure approx 3½"/9cm x 12"/30.5cm.

RECTANGLE 13

With D, ch 70.

Row 1 Hdc in 2nd ch from hook (counts as 1 hdc), hdc in each ch across. Ch 2, turn.

Row 2 Hdc in each hdc across. Ch 2, turn.

Rows 3—6 Rep row 1. Fasten off. Piece should measure approx 15"/38cm x 1½"/4cm.

EDGING

With D, sc around each rectangle, working into the foundation ch, top row and post sts on each side.

FINISHING

Assemble rectangles according to diagram and pin pieces together. Whipstitch into each single crochet around borders of rectangles to join.

Block shawl lightly to measurements. Weave in ends.

Assembly Diagram

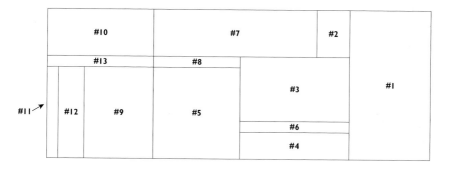

ARAN SHAWL

Buttons and bobbles

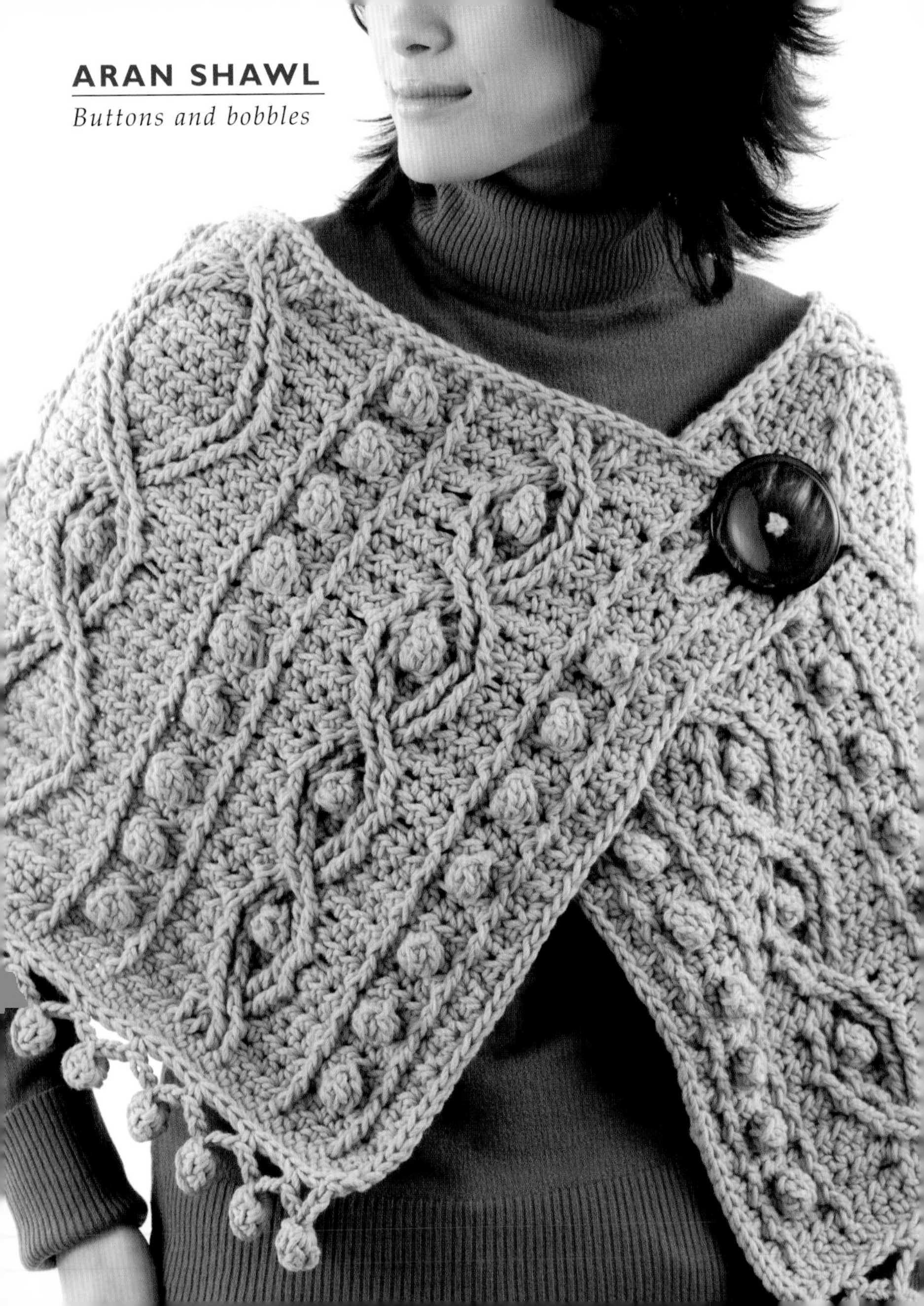

■ ■ ■ ▶

Show off your crochet cable skills with Brett Bara's beautifully crafted wrap. It fits snugly around the shoulders and fastens with a sassy, supersized button.

SIZES
Instructions are written for one size.

FINISHED MEASUREMENTS
■ Approx 17½"/44.5cm x 50"/127cm

MATERIALS
■ 9 3½oz/100g hanks (each approx 100yd/91m) of Blue Sky Alpacas *Worsted Hand Dyes* (alpaca/wool) in #2009 tan ④

■ Size K/10½ (6.5mm) crochet hook *or size to obtain gauge*

GAUGE
10 sts and 10 rows to 4"/10cm over hdc using size K/10½ (6.5mm) hook.
Take time to check gauge.

Notes
1 Gauge is not critical for this pattern.
2 Always sk st behind front post sts.

STITCH GLOSSARY
Bobble Work 5 dc in next st, drop lp from hook, insert hook in top of 1st dc and pull loop through.

STITCH PATTERNS
Bobble panel
(worked over 5 sts)

Row 1 (RS) Fpdc in fpdc 2 rows below, hdc in next 3 hdc, fpdc in fpdc 2 rows below.
Row 2 Hdc in each sts across.
Row 3 Fpdc in hdc 2 rows below, hdc in next hdc, bobble in next hdc, hdc in next hdc, fpdc in hdc 2 rows below.
Row 4 Rep row 2.
Rep rows 1–4.

Small cable panel
(worked over 11 sts)
Row 1 (RS) Hdc in next 3 hdc, sk next 3 hdc, fptr in next 2 hdc 2 rows below, hdc in 3rd skipped hdc, fptr in 1st 2 skipped hdc 2 rows below, hdc in next 3 hdc.
Row 2 and all WS rows Hdc in each st across.
Row 3 Hdc in next 2 hdc, fptr in 2 fptr below, hdc in next 3 hdc, fptr in 2 fptr below, hdc in next 2 hdc.
Row 5 Hdc in next hdc, fptr in 2 fptr below, hdc in next 2 hdc, bobble in next hdc, hdc in next 2 hdc, fptr in 2 fptr below, hdc in next hdc.
Row 7 Rep row 3.
Row 8 Rep row 2.
Rep rows 1–8.

Large cable panel
(worked over 13 sts)
Row 1 Hdc in next 4 hdc, sk next 3 hdc, fptr in next 2 hdc 2 rows below, hdc in 3rd skipped hdc, fptr in 1st 2 skipped hdc's 2 rows below, hdc in next 4 hdc.

Row 2 and all WS rows Hdc in each st across.

Row 3 Hdc in next 3 hdc, fptr in 2 fptr below, hdc in next 3 hdc, fptr in 2 fptr below, hdc in next 3 hdc.

Row 5 Hdc in next 2 hdc, fptr in 2 fptr below, hdc in next 5 hdc, fptr in 2 fptr below, hdc in next 2 hdc.

Row 7 Hdc in 1st hdc, fptr in 2 fptr below, hdc in next 7 hdc, fptr in 2 fptr below, hdc in next hdc.

Row 9 Rep row 5.

Row 11 Rep row 3.

Row 13 Rep row 1.

Row 15 Rep row 3.

Row 17 Hdc in next 2 hdc, fptr in 2 fptr below, hdc in next 2 hdc, bobble in next hdc, hdc in next 2 hdc, fptr in 2 fptr below, hdc in next 2 hdc.

Row 19 Rep row 3.

Rows 21–32 Rep rows 1–12.

Rows 33–34 Rep rows 1 and 2.

SHAWL

Ch 127.

Foundation row Hdc in 3rd ch from hook and each ch across—125 hdc. Ch 2, turn.

Establish pat Hdc in 1st hdc, * + fpdc in next hdc 2 rows below, hdc in next 3 hdc, fpdc in next hdc 2 rows below **, hdc in next 3 hdc, fpdc around next 2 hdc 2 rows below, hdc in next hdc, fpdc around next 2 hdc 2 rows below, hdc in next 3 hdc, rep from * to ** , hdc in next 4 hdc, fpdc around next 2 hdc 2 rows below, hdc in next hdc, fpdc around next 2 hdc 2 rows below, hdc in next 4 hdc ++, rep from + to ++ 2 more times, rep from * to ** , hdc in next 3 hdc, fpdc around next 2 hdc 2 rows below, hdc in next hdc, fpdc around next 2 hdc 2 rows below, hdc in next 3 hdc, rep from * to ** , hdc in last hdc.

Next row Hdc in each hdc across. Ch 2, turn.

Row 1 Hdc in 1st hdc, *work row 1 of: bobble panel, small cable panel, bobble panel, large cable panel ** ; rep from * to ** 2 more times, work row 1 of: bobble panel, small cable panel, bobble panel, hdc in last hdc. Ch 2, turn.

Row 2 and all WS rows Hdc in each st across. Ch 2, turn.

Continue in established pats until 7 reps of bobble panel have been worked.

Note Continue in established pats across row making a buttonhole on the 8th rep of bobble panel as follows:

Next 2 rows Continue to work all panels across row as established.

Next row (RS) Divide work on this row (row 3) of 1st bobble panel to make vertical buttonhole as follows: hdc in 1st hdc of row, fpdc in fpdc below, hdc in next hdc, ch 2, turn. Continue to follow pat working this narrow strip for 7 rows, ending with a WS row. Do not fasten off. Return to dividing row and attach a separate ball of yarn, sk 1 hdc, then continue to work across length of wrap in established pat. Continue to follow pat for 7 rows until even with narrow strip, ending with a WS row. Fasten off.

EDGING

Using working yarn from beg of narrow strip, work across entire length of wrap same as foundation row. Ch 2, turn.

Next row Hdc in each st across. Fasten off.

BORDER

Rnd 1 With RS facing, beg at top right corner, join yarn with a sl st and sc around wrap, working sc in each hdc across top edge, sc along side edges, sc in each free loop of foundation ch and 3 sc in each corner. Ch 1, turn.

Rnd 2 With WS facing, sl st in each sc from previous rnd. Fasten off.

BOBBLE TRIM

With RS facing, beg at bottom left corner, join yarn with sl st and sc in same st as joining. *ch 6, work 5 dc in 3rd ch from hook, drop lp from hook, insert hook in top of 1st dc and pull lp through. Drop lp again, insert hook from front to back in 3rd ch from hook (same ch where 5 dc were made) and pull lp through ch (bobble made). Ch 3, sk 3 sl sts, sc in next sl st; rep from * to end of bottom edge. Fasten off.

FINISHING

Working inside the buttonhole opening, sc evenly around opening. Ch1, sl st in each sc around. Fasten off.

Sew button to corner of wrap opposite buttonhole. Position button so that wrap will fit correctly around shoulders when closed. Weave in all ends.

RESOURCES

Write to the yarn companies listed below for purchasing and mail-order information.

Alchemy Yarns of Transformation
P.O. Box 1080
Sebastopol, CA 95473
www.alchemyyarns.com

Berroco, Inc.
P.O. Box 367
14 Elmdale Road
Uxbridge, MA 01569
www.berroco.com

Blue Sky Alpacas
PO Box 387
St. Francis, MN 55070
www.blueskyalpacas.com

Brown Sheep Company
100662 County Road 16
Mitchell, NE 69357
www.brownsheep.com

Classic Elite Yarns
122 Western Avenue
Lowell, MA 01851
www.classiceliteyarns.com

Coats & Clark
3430 Toringdon Way
Suite 301
Charlotte, NC 28277
www.coatsandclark.com

Crystal Palace Yarns
160 23rd Street
Richmond, CA 94804
www.crystalpalaceyarns.com

Fiesta Yarns
5401 San Diego NE
Albuquerque, NM 87112
www.fiestayarns.com

Filatura Di Crosa
distributed by
Tahki Stacy Charles, Inc.

GGH
distributed by
Muench Yarns

JCA, Inc.
35 Scales Lane
Townsend, MA 01469
www.jcacrafts.com

Knit One, Crochet Too, Inc.
91 Tandberg Trail, Unit 6
Windham, ME 04062
www.knitonecrochettoo.com

Lion Brand Yarn
34 West 15th Street
New York, NY 10011
www.lionbrand.com

Muench Yarns, Inc.
1323 Scott Street
Petaluma, CA 94954-1135
www.myyarns.com

Nashua Handknits
Distributed by
Westminster Fibers, Inc.

Plymouth Yarn Co.
P.O. Box 28
Bristol, PA 19007
www.plymouthyarn.com

Red Heart
distributed by
Coats & Clark

Reynolds
distributed by
JCA, Inc.

Rowan Yarns
distributed by
Westminster Fibers, Inc.
www.knitrowan.com

Tahki Stacy Charles, Inc.
70-30 80th Street
Building #36
Ridgewood, NY 11385
www.tahkistacycharles.com

Tahki Yarns
distributed by
Tahki•Stacy Charles, Inc.

Trendsetter Yarns
16745 Saticoy Street,
Suite #101
Van Nuys, CA 91406
www.trendsetteryarns.com

Westminster Fibers
165 Ledge Street
Nashua, NH 03060
www.westminsterfibers.com

U.K. RESOURCES

Not all yarns used in this book are available in the U.K. For yarns not available, make a comparable substitute or contact the U.S. manufacturer for purchasing and mail-order information.

Green Lane Mill
Holmfirth
HD9 2DX England
www.knitrowan.com

CANADIAN RESOURCES

Write to U.S. resources for mail-order availability of yarns not listed.

Koigu Wool Designs
P.O. Box 158
563295 Glenelg Holland Townline
Chatsworth, Ontario
Canada N0H 1G0
www.koigu.com

VOGUE KNITTING CROCHETED SHAWLS

Editorial Director
ELAINE SILVERSTEIN

Book Division Manager
ERICA SMITH

Executive Editor
CARLA S. SCOTT

Associate Editor
AMANDA KEISER

Art Director
CHI LING MOY

Associate Art Director
SHEENA T. PAUL

Yarn Editor
TANIS GRAY

Instructions Editor
RITA GREENFEDER

Instructions Proofreader
MARY KATHRYN SIMON

Copy Editor
KRISTINA SIGLER

Photography
JACK DEUTSCH STUDIO

Photo Stylist
LAURA MAFFEO

Vice President, Publisher
TRISHA MALCOLM

Production Manager
DAVID JOINNIDES

Creative Director
JOE VIOR

President
ART JOINNIDES

Look for these other titles in
THE *VOGUE KNITTING ON THE GO!* SERIES...